William Bright

The Definitions of the Catholic Faith

And Canons of Discipline of the First Four General Councils of the Universal Church. Third Edition

William Bright

The Definitions of the Catholic Faith
And Canons of Discipline of the First Four General Councils of the Universal Church.
Third Edition

ISBN/EAN: 9783337259365

Printed in Europe, USA, Canada, Australia, Japan

Cover: Foto ©Lupo / pixelio.de

More available books at **www.hansebooks.com**

THE DEFINITIONS

OF

THE CATHOLIC FAITH,

AND

CANONS OF DISCIPLINE

OF THE

FIRST FOUR GENERAL COUNCILS OF THE UNIVERSAL CHURCH:

IN GREEK AND ENGLISH.

Συμεὼν ἐξηγήσατο . . .
διὸ ἐγὼ κρίνω.
Acts of the Apostles, xv. 14, 19.

THIRD EDITION.

Oxford and London:
JAMES PARKER AND CO.
1874.

ADVERTISEMENT.

THE Decrees of the First Four General Councils being declared as authoritative by the Act of Parliament, and having been re-affirmed at the Conference of Archbishops and Bishops of the Anglican Communion assembled at Lambeth in the present year (1867), as part of the Rule of Faith of the United Church of England and Ireland; it has been thought well to place these important documents within easy reach of English readers.

The Greek text is that which has been followed by Dr. Routh, "Script. Eccl. Opusc.," ed. 1832. The English version is based on that printed in J. Johnson's "Clergyman's Vade Mecum," ed. 1709; with some additions, for which the Editor is mainly indebted to Mr. Hammond's translation, ed. Oxford, 1843. The notes are taken chiefly from the above-named sources. Reference has also been made to the English version of the Nicene Canons printed at the end of "A History of the Church, A.D. 313—451," by the Rev. W. Bright, M.A., Fellow of University College, and since Regius Professor of Ecclesiastical History in Oxford.

W. H. B.

Oxford.

CONTENTS.

	PAGE
NICENE CREED	3
——— CANONS	5
SYNODAL EPISTLE OF THE COUNCIL OF CONSTANTINOPLE	23
CONSTANTINOPOLITAN CANONS	25
CREED OF CONSTANTINOPLE	35
SYNODAL EPISTLE OF THE COUNCIL OF EPHESUS	37
EPHESINE CANONS	39
CHALCEDON CANONS	49
——————— DEFINITION OF THE FAITH	81

THE DECREES

OF

THE FIRST FOUR GENERAL COUNCILS

OF

THE CATHOLIC CHURCH.

SYMBOLUM NICÆNUM,
AD EXEMPLAR QUOD EXTAT IN ACTIS CHALCEDONENSIS CONCILII.

ΠΙΣΤΕΥΟΜΕΝ εἰς ἕνα Θεὸν πατέρα, παντοκράτορα, πάντων ὁρατῶν τε καὶ ἀοράτων ποιητήν. Καὶ εἰς ἕνα Κύριον Ἰησοῦν Χριστὸν, τὸν υἱὸν τοῦ Θεοῦ, γεννηθέντα ἐκ τοῦ πατρὸς, μονογενῆ, τουτέστιν ἐκ τῆς οὐσίας τοῦ πατρός· Θεὸν ἐκ Θεοῦ, φῶς ἐκ φῶτος, Θεὸν ἀληθινὸν ἐκ Θεοῦ ἀληθινοῦ, γεννηθέντα οὐ ποιηθέντα, ὁμοούσιον τῷ πατρί. Δι' οὗ τὰ πάντα ἐγένετο, τάτε ἐν τῷ οὐρανῷ καὶ τὰ ἐν τῇ γῇ· τὸν δι' ἡμᾶς τοὺς ἀνθρώπους, καὶ διὰ τὴν ἡμετέραν σωτηρίαν κατελθόντα, καὶ σαρκωθέντα, καὶ ἐνανθρωπήσαντα· παθόντα, καὶ ἀναστάντα τῇ τρίτῃ ἡμέρᾳ· ἀνελθόντα εἰς τοὺς οὐράνους. καὶ πάλιν ἐρχόμενον κρῖναι ζῶντας καὶ νεκρούς. Καὶ εἰς τὸ Πνεῦμα τὸ ἅγιον. Τοὺς δὲ λέγοντας· ἦν ποτε ὅτε οὐκ ἦν, καὶ πρὶν γεννηθῆναι οὐκ ἦν, καὶ ὅτι ἐξ οὐκ ὄντων ἐγένετο, ἢ ἐξ ἑτέρας ὑποστάσεως ἢ οὐσίας φάσκοντας εἶναι, ἢ τρεπτὸν, ἢ ἀλλοιωτὸν τὸν υἱὸν τοῦ Θεοῦ, τούτους ἀναθεματίζει ἡ καθολικὴ καὶ ἀποστολικὴ ἐκκλησία.

THE NICENE CREED.

WE believe in one God, the Father, Almighty, Maker of all things visible and invisible:

And in one Lord Jesus Christ, the ~~only-begotten~~ Son of God, begotten of the Father, only begotten, that is, of the substance of the Father, God of God, Light of Light, Very God of very God, begotten, not made, consubstantial with the Father. By whom all things were made both in heaven and earth; who for us men and for our salvation came down, and was incarnate, and was made man. He suffered, and rose again the third day, and ascended into heaven; and shall come again to judge the quick and the dead.

And in the Holy Ghost,

And for them that say, concerning the Son of God, There was a time when He was not; and, He was not before He was produced; and, He was produced from things that are not; and, He is of another substance, or essence, or that the Son of God is subject to conversion or mutation, the Catholic and Apostolic Church saith, Let them be anathema.

CANONES
NICÆNI CONCILII UNIVERSALIS.
A.D. 325.

Κανόνες τῶν τριακοσίων δέκα καὶ ὀκτὼ ἁγίων πατέρων τῶν ἐν Νικαίᾳ συνελθόντων.

ΚΑΝΩΝ Α.

ΕΙΤΙΣ ἐν νόσῳ ὑπὸ ἰατρῶν ἐχειρουργήθη, ἢ ὑπὸ βαρβάρων ἐξετμήθη, οὗτος μενέτω ἐν τῷ κλήρῳ. εἰ δέ τις ὑγιαίνων ἑαυτὸν ἐξέτεμεν, τοῦτον καὶ ἐν τῷ κλήρῳ ἐξεταζόμενον πεπαῦσθαι προσήκει· καὶ ἐκ τοῦ δεῦρο μηδένα τῶν τοιούτων χρῆναι προάγεσθαι. ὥσπερ δὲ τοῦτο πρόδηλον, ὅτι περὶ τῶν ἐπιτηδευόντων τὸ πρᾶγμα καὶ τολμώντων ἑαυτοὺς ἐκτέμνειν εἴρηται. οὕτως εἴτινες ὑπὸ βαρβάρων ἢ δεσποτῶν εὐνουχίσθησαν, εὑρίσκοιντο δὲ ἄλλως ἄξιοι, τοὺς τοιούτους εἰς κλῆρον προσίεται ὁ κανών.

ΚΑΝΩΝ Β.

Ἐπειδὴ πολλὰ ἤτοι ὑπὸ ἀνάγκης ἢ ἄλλως ἐπειγομένων τῶν ἀνθρώπων ἐγένετο παρὰ τὸν κανόνα τὸν ἐκκλησιαστικόν, ὥστε ἀνθρώπους ἀπὸ ἐθνικοῦ βίου ἄρτι προσελθόντας τῇ πίστει, καὶ ἐν ὀλίγῳ χρόνῳ κατηχηθέντας, εὐθὺς ἐπὶ τὸ πνευματικὸν λουτρὸν ἄγειν, καὶ ἅμα τῷ βαπτισθῆναι προσάγειν εἰς ἐπισκοπήν, ἢ εἰς πρεσβυτέριον· καλῶς ἔδοξεν ἔχειν τοῦ λοιποῦ μηδὲν τοιοῦτο γίνεσθαι. καὶ γὰρ καὶ χρόνου δεῖ τῷ κατηχου-

THE CANONS
OF THE NICENE GENERAL COUNCIL.

THE CANONS OF THE 318 HOLY FATHERS GATHERED TOGETHER AT NICÆA [a].

I.
OF EUNUCHS.

IF any one be made an eunuch by a physician for any disease, or by the barbarians, or by any one whom he served as a slave, he may continue or be admitted into the clergy; but not if he makes himself an eunuch, when he was a sound man [b].

II.
BISHOPS ARE NOT TO LAY HANDS SUDDENLY ON ANY.

Because many things have been done contrary to Church Rule, insomuch that some men have lately been proselyted to the faith from a heathen course of life, and having for a while been catechumens have been presently baptized, and thereupon preferred to be Bishops, or Priests; It is decreed, that nothing of the sort be done for the future; for a man should stay a Catechumen for some time, and after baptism be fully

---

[a] This Council was assembled for the purpose of determining the faith which had been attacked by Arius and his followers. The Bishop of Rome was represented at it by the Priests Vitus and Vincentius. Alexander, Bishop of Alexandria, Eustathius of Antioch, and Hosius of Corduba were Presidents of the Council. The Canons of Sardica, which are an appendix to those of Nice, are translated in the "Clergyman's Vade Mecum."

[b] St. Matt. xviii. 8, 9, xix. 12. See Socrates ii. 21.

μένῳ, καὶ μετὰ τὸ βάπτισμα δοκιμασίας πλείονος. σαφὲς γὰρ τὸ ἀποστολικὸν γράμμα τὸ λέγον, Μηδὲ νεόφυτον, ἵνα μὴ τυφωθεὶς εἰς κρίμα ἐμπέσῃ καὶ παγίδα τοῦ διαβόλου· εἰ δὲ προϊόντος τοῦ χρόνου ψυχικόν τι ἁμάρτημα εὑρεθείη περὶ τὸ πρόσωπον, καὶ ἐλέγχοιτο ὑπὸ δύο ἢ τριῶν μαρτύρων, πεπαύσθω ὁ τοιοῦτος τοῦ κλήρου. ὁ δὲ παρὰ ταῦτα ποιῶν, ὡς ὑπεναντία τῇ μεγάλῃ συνόδῳ θρασυνόμενος, αὐτὸς κινδυνεύσει περὶ τὸν κλῆρον.

ΚΑΝΩΝ Γ.

Ἀπηγόρευσεν καθόλου ἡ μεγάλη σύνοδος. μήτε ἐπισκόπῳ, μήτε πρεσβυτέρῳ, μήτε διακόνῳ, μήτε ὅλως τινὶ τῶν ἐν τῷ κλήρῳ, ἐξεῖναι συνείσακτον ἔχειν· πλὴν εἰμὴ ἄρα μητέρα, ἢ ἀδελφήν, ἢ θείαν, ἢ ἃ μόνα πρόσωπα πᾶσαν ὑποψίαν διαπέφευγεν.

ΚΑΝΩΝ Δ.

Ἐπίσκοπον προσήκει μάλιστα μὲν ὑπὸ πάντων τῶν ἐν τῇ ἐπαρχίᾳ καθίστασθαι. εἰ δὲ δυσχερὲς εἴη τὸ τοιοῦτο, ἢ διὰ κατεπείγουσαν ἀνάγκην, ἢ διὰ μῆκος ὁδοῦ· ἐξ ἅπαντος τρεῖς ἐπὶ τὸ αὐτὸ συναγομένους, συμψήφων γινομένων καὶ τῶν ἀπόντων καὶ συντιθεμένων διὰ γραμμάτων, τότε τὴν χειροτονίαν ποιεῖσθαι. τὸ δὲ κῦρος τῶν γινομένων δίδοσθαι καθ' ἑκάστην ἐπαρχίαν τῷ μητροπολίτῃ.

ΚΑΝΩΝ Ε.

Περὶ τῶν ἀκοινωνήτων γενομένων, εἴτε τῶν ἐν τῷ κλήρῳ εἴτε τῶν ἐν λαϊκῷ τάγματι ὑπὸ τῶν καθ' ἑκάστην ἐπαρχίαν

proved: for the Apostolic decree is clear:—"Not a neophyte, lest being puffed up, he fall into condemnation and the snare of the devil [c];"—and if any after a long time be convicted of any sensual sin, let him be dismissed from the clergy. [The Bishop] that does otherwise, shall do it at the peril of his Orders, as one that dare oppose the great Synod.

III.
OF THE HOUSEHOLDS OF THE CLERGY.

THE great Synod strictly forbids Bishops, Priests, and Deacons, and all clergymen [d], to retain any woman in their houses, under pretence of her being a disciple [e] to them; but only a mother, sister, aunt, or other unsuspected person.

IV.
OF THE APPOINTMENT OF BISHOPS.

A BISHOP ought to be constituted [f] by all the Bishops that belong to the province; but if this be not practicable, either through pressing necessity, or the length of the journey, three must by all means meet; and when they have the consent of those that are absent, signified by letter, then let them perform the consecration; and the ratification of what is done must be allowed in each Province to the Metropolitan.

V.
CONCERNING EXCOMMUNICATE PERSONS.

LET sentence according to Canon [g] prevail, that clergymen or laymen, being excommunicated by some, be not

---

[c] 1 Tim. iii. 6. [d] The existence of minor orders is here implied. Can. Chalc. xiv. note.
[e] See Bingham, vi. 2, 13. [f] That is—*elected and appointed.*
[g] The 10th, 12th, and 13th Apostolic Canons.

ἐπισκόπων, κρατείτω ἡ γνώμη κατὰ τὸν κανόνα τὸν διαγορεύοντα, τοὺς ὑφ' ἑτέρων ἀποβληθέντας, ὑφ' ἑτέρων μὴ προσίεσθαι. ἐξεταζέσθω δέ, μὴ μικροψυχίᾳ ἢ φιλονεικίᾳ, ἤ τινι τοιαύτῃ ἀηδίᾳ τοῦ ἐπισκόπου ἀποσυνάγωγοι γεγένηνται. ἵνα οὖν τοῦτο τὴν πρέπουσαν ἐξέτασιν λαμβάνῃ, καλῶς ἔχειν ἔδοξεν ἑκάστου ἐνιαυτοῦ καθ' ἑκάστην ἐπαρχίαν δὶς τοῦ ἔτους συνόδους γίνεσθαι. ἵνα κοινῇ πάντων τῶν ἐπισκόπων τῆς ἐπαρχίας ἐπὶ τὸ αὐτὸ συναγομένων τὰ τοιαῦτα ζητήματα ἐξετάζοιτο· καὶ οὕτως οἱ ὁμολογουμένως προσκεκρουκότες τῷ ἐπισκόπῳ κατὰ λόγον ἀκοινώνητοι παρὰ πᾶσιν εἶναι δόξωσι, μέχρις ἂν τῷ κοινῷ τῶν ἐπισκόπων δόξῃ τὴν φιλανθρωποτέραν ὑπὲρ αὐτῶν ἐκθέσθαι ψῆφον· αἱ δὲ σύνοδοι γινέσθωσαν, μία μὲν πρὸ τῆς τεσσαρακοστῆς, ἵνα πάσης μικροψυχίας ἀναιρουμένης, τὸ δῶρον καθαρὸν προσφέρηται τῷ Θεῷ. δευτέρα δὲ περὶ τὸν τοῦ μετοπώρου καιρόν.

ΚΑΝΩΝ ϛ'.

Τὰ ἀρχαῖα ἔθη κρατείτω, τὰ ἐν Αἰγύπτῳ καὶ Λιβύῃ καὶ Πενταπόλει, ὥστε τὸν Ἀλεξανδρείας ἐπίσκοπον πάντων τούτων ἔχειν τὴν ἐξουσίαν. ἐπειδὴ καὶ τῷ ἐν τῇ Ῥώμῃ ἐπισκόπῳ τοῦτο σύνηθές ἐστιν. ὁμοίως δὲ καὶ κατὰ τὴν Ἀντιόχειαν καὶ ἐν ταῖς ἄλλαις ἐπαρχίαις, τὰ πρεσβεῖα σώζεσθαι ταῖς ἐκκλησίαις. καθόλου δὲ πρόδηλον ἐκεῖνο, ὅτι εἴ τις χωρὶς γνώμης τοῦ μητροπολίτου γένοιτο ἐπίσκοπος, τὸν τοιοῦτον ἡ μεγάλη σύνοδος ὥρισε μὴ δεῖν εἶναι ἐπίσκοπον. ἐὰν μέν τοι τῇ κοινῇ

received by others: and let examination be made whether any have been excommunicated by the captiousness, or party spirit, or any such like unpleasantness of the Bishop. And that this inquiry be duly made, it seems good that two Synods should be held in the year; that such questions may be entered into at an assembly of all the Bishops, so that those who have confessedly offended against the Bishop may appear excommunicated by them all; until by the same authority a more lenient sentence is passed upon them.

Let one Synod be held before Lent, that so, all animosity being removed, the pure Gift[h] may be offered to God; the other about autumn.

VI.
Of the Privileges of certain Provinces.

LET the ancient customs prevail, namely, those in Egypt, Libya, and Pentapolis: that the Bishop of Alexandria have power over all these, since the same is customary for the Bishop of Rome. Likewise, in Antioch and other provinces, let the privileges be secured to the Churches. This is manifest as any thing at all, that if any be made a Bishop, without consent of his Metropolitan[i], this great Synod has determined, that such a one ought not to be Bishop. If any two or three, out of affectation of dispute, do contradict the

[h] On the Antiquity of Lent see Bingham, xxi. 1, and a fragment of a letter of St. Irenæus to Pope Victor, ap. Euseb. Hist., v. 24. This care for the worthy celebration of the Eucharist (Malachi i. 11; St. Matt. v. 23) points to the fact that the possibility of the Catholic Church being so divided, as that one part should not be in communion with all, had not then been conceived.

[i] It is to be noted that the authority of Metropolitans is much older than this Synod. In this and other points of jurisdiction reference is made to the case of Meletius, whose so-called schism lasted fifty-six years.

πάντων ψήφῳ εὐλόγῳ οὔσῃ, καὶ κατὰ κανόνα ἐκκλησιαστικὸν, δύο ἢ τρεῖς δι' οἰκείαν φιλονεικίαν ἀντιλέγωσι, κρατείτω ἡ τῶν πλειόνων ψῆφος.

ΚΑΝΩΝ Ζ.

Ἐπειδὴ συνήθεια κεκράτηκε καὶ παράδοσις ἀρχαία, ὥστε τὸν ἐν Αἰλίᾳ ἐπίσκοπον τιμᾶσθαι, ἐχέτω τὴν ἀκολουθίαν τῆς τιμῆς, τῇ μητροπόλει σωζομένου τοῦ οἰκείου ἀξιώματος.

ΚΑΝΩΝ Η.

Περὶ τῶν ὀνομαζόντων μὲν ἑαυτοὺς Καθαρούς ποτε, προσερχομένων δὲ τῇ καθολικῇ καὶ ἀποστολικῇ ἐκκλησίᾳ, ἔδοξε τῇ ἁγίᾳ καὶ μεγάλῃ συνόδῳ, ὥστε χειροθετουμένους αὐτοὺς μένειν οὕτως ἐν τῷ κλήρῳ. πρὸ πάντων δὲ τοῦτο ὁμολογῆσαι αὐτοὺς ἐγγράφως προσήκει, ὅτι συνθήσονται καὶ ἀκολουθήσουσι τοῖς τῆς καθολικῆς καὶ ἀποστολικῆς ἐκκλησίας δόγμασι, τοῦτ' ἔστι, καὶ διγάμοις κοινωνεῖν, καὶ τοῖς ἐν τῷ διωγμῷ παραπεπτωκόσιν· ἐφ' ὧν καὶ χρόνος τέτακται, καὶ καιρὸς ὥρισται· ὥστε αὐτοὺς ἀκολουθεῖν, ἐν πᾶσι, τοῖς δόγμασι τῆς καθολικῆς ἐκκλησίας. ἔνθα μὲν οὖν πάντες (for. πάντῃ) εἴτε ἐν κώμαις, εἴτε ἐν πόλεσιν αὐτοὶ μόνοι εὑρίσκοιντο χειροτονηθέντες, οἱ εὑρισκόμενοι, ἐν τῷ κλήρῳ ἔσονται ἐν τῷ αὐτῷ σχήματι. εἰ δὲ τοῦ τῆς καθολικῆς ἐκκλησίας ἐπισκόπου ἢ πρεσβυτέρου ὄντος προσέρχονταί τινες, πρόδηλον, ὡς ὁ μὲν ἐπίσκοπος τῆς ἐκκλησίας ἕξει τὸ ἀξίωμα τοῦ ἐπισκόπου· ὁ δὲ ὀνομαζόμενος παρὰ τοῖς λεγομένοις Καθαροῖς ἐπίσκοπος, τὴν τοῦ πρεσβυτέρου τιμὴν ἕξει. πλὴν εἰ μὴ ἄρα δοκοίη τῷ ἐπισκόπῳ τῆς τιμῆς

suffrage of the generality, when duly passed according to Ecclesiastical Canon, let the votes of the majority prevail.

VII.
OF THE BISHOP OF JERUSALEM.

SAVING to the Metropolis its proper dignity, let the Bishop of Ælia[k] have the next place of precedence[1]; because custom and ancient tradition have obtained that he should be honoured.

VIII.
CONCERNING THE RECONCILIATION OF CERTAIN SCHISMATICS.

As to those who call themselves Puritans[m], if they come over to the Catholic and Apostolic Church, the holy Synod decrees, that they who are ordained shall continue in the clergy, having first professed in writing that they will adhere to the decrees of the Catholic Church; that is, that they will communicate with those that have married a second time, and such as having lapsed under persecution have had a certain time of penance allotted them: and that they will follow in all things the decrees of the Catholic Church. Where, therefore, none but they are found to be ordained in any city or village, they shall remain in the same Order; but if any come over where there is a Bishop or Priest of the Catholic Church, it is clear that the Bishop of the Church ought to retain his dignity: and he that had been named Bishop by the Puritans, shall have the honour of a Priest, unless the Bishop think

---

[k] The Roman Jerusalem.   [1] 1 Tim. v. 17. Can. Chalc. xxix. note.
[m] The Novatians, who had true orders, and, with the exception of the denials of reconciliation above mentioned, were orthodox.

τοῦ ὀνόματος αὐτὸν μετέχειν. εἰ δὲ τοῦτο αὐτῷ μὴ ἀρέσκοι, ἐπινοήσει τόπον ἢ χωρεπισκόπου ἢ πρεσβυτέρου ὑπὲρ τοῦ ἐν τῷ κλήρῳ ὅλως δοκεῖν εἶναι, ἵνα μὴ ἐν τῇ πόλει δύο ἐπίσκοποι ὦσιν.

ΚΑΝΩΝ Θ.

Εἴ τινες ἀνεξετάστως προήχθησαν πρεσβύτεροι, ἢ ἀνακρινόμενοι ὡμολόγησαν τὰ ἁμαρτήμενα αὐτοῖς, καὶ ὁμολογησάντων αὐτῶν παρὰ κανόνα κινούμενοι οἱ ἄνθρωποι, τοῖς τοιούτοις χεῖρα ἐπιτεθείκασιν· τούτους ὁ κανὼν οὐ προσίεται. τὸ γὰρ ἀνεπίληπτον ἐκδικεῖ ἡ καθολικὴ ἐκκλησία.

ΚΑΝΩΝ Ι.

Ὅσοι προεχειρίσθησαν τῶν παραπεπτωκότων κατὰ ἄγνοιαν, ἢ καὶ προειδότων τῶν προχειρισαμένων, τοῦτο οὐ προκρίνει τῷ κανόνι τῷ ἐκκλησιαστικῷ. γνωσθέντες γὰρ καθαιροῦνται.

ΚΑΝΩΝ ΙΑ.

Περὶ τῶν παραβάντων χωρὶς ἀνάγκης, ἢ χωρὶς ἀφαιρέσεως ὑπαρχόντων, ἢ χωρὶς κινδύνου, ἤ τινος τοιούτου, ὃ γέγονεν ἐπὶ τῆς τυραννίδος Λικινίου· ἔδοξε τῇ συνόδῳ, εἰ καὶ ἀνάξιοι ἦσαν φιλανθρωπίας, ὅμως χρηστεύσασθαι εἰς αὐτούς. ὅσοι οὖν

fit to impart to him the nominal honour [of a Bishop]. Otherwise he shall provide for him the place of a village ᵃ Bishop or Priest, that so there may not be two Bishops in one city.

IX.
Concerning the Irregular Ordination of Priests.

Whoever have been promoted to be Priests without examination, or having been examined have confessed their sins; and yet men, acting contrary to the Canon, have laid hands on them; such as these the Canon does not admit of. For the Catholic Church justifies [only] that which is blameless.

X.
Of the Ordination of the Lapsed.

Whatever persons having lapsed, have afterwards been ordained through ignorance, or even with the knowledge of those who ordained them, this shall not prejudice the Canon of the Church; for being discovered they shall be deposed.

XI.
Concerning the Penance of the Lapsed Laity.

As to those who have transgressed without necessity, loss of estate, and the like, during the tyranny of Licinius ᵇ, the Synod has decreed that although they deserve not clemency, they shall be dealt with mercifully. Therefore as many of them as do ingenuously

---

ᵃ A Chorepiscopus, whose privileges varied in different places; they might ordain the minor orders of readers, subdeacons, &c., and confirm in country churches. By Concil. Antioch., Can. x., one Bishop only was required to ordain a Chorepiscopus. "The rule of one Bishop only in a city was of universal observance in the Church from the very beginning."   ᵇ A.D. 320-4.

γνησίως μεταμελῶνται, τρία ἔτη ἐν ἀκροωμενοις ποιήσουσιν οἱ πιστοί· καὶ ἑπτὰ ἔτη ὑποπεσοῦνται. δύο δὲ ἔτη χωρὶς προσφορᾶς κοινωνήσουσι τῷ λαῷ τῶν προσευχῶν.

ΚΑΝΩΝ ΙΒ.

Οἱ δὲ προσκληθέντες μὲν ὑπὸ τῆς χάριτος καὶ τὴν πρώτην ὁρμὴν ἐνδειξάμενοι, καὶ ἀποθέμενοι τὰς ζώνας, μετὰ δὲ ταῦτα ἐπὶ τὸν οἰκεῖον ἔμετον ἀναδραμόντες ὡς κύνες, ὥς τινας καὶ ἀργύρια πρόεσθαι, καὶ βενεφικίοις κατορθῶσαι τὸ ἀναστρατεύσασθαι· οὗτοι δέκα ἔτη ὑποπιπτέτωσαν, μετὰ τὸν τῆς τριετοῦς ἀκροάσεως χρόνον. ἐφ' ἅπασι δὲ τούτοις, προσήκει ἐξετάζειν τὴν προαίρεσιν καὶ τὸ εἶδος τῆς μετανοίας. ὅσοι μὲν γὰρ καὶ φόβῳ καὶ δάκρυσι καὶ ὑπομονῇ καὶ ἀγαθοεργίαις, τὴν ἐπιστροφὴν ἔργῳ καὶ οὐ σχήματι ἐπιδείκνυνται, οὗτοι πληρώσαντες τὸν χρόνον τὸν ὡρισμένον τῆς ἀκροάσεως, εἰκότως τῶν εὐχῶν κοινωνήσουσι, μετὰ τοῦ ἐξεῖναι τῷ ἐπισκόπῳ καὶ φιλανθρωπότερόν τι περὶ αὐτῶν βουλεύσασθαι, ὅσοι δὲ ἀδιαφόρως ἤνεγκαν, καὶ τὸ σχῆμα τοῦ εἰσιέναι εἰς τὴν ἐκκλησίαν ἀρκεῖν ἑαυτοῖς ἡγήσαντο πρὸς τὴν ἐπιστρέφειαν, ἐξ ἅπαντος πληρούτωσαν τὸν χρόνον.

ΚΑΝΩΝ ΙΓ.

Περὶ δὲ τῶν ἐξοδευόντων, ὁ παλαιὸς καὶ κανονικὸς νόμος φυλαχθήσεται καὶ νῦν, ὥστε εἴτις ἐξοδεύοι, τοῦ τελευταίου

repent, let them if they were [formerly] communicants, spend three years amongst the hearers; for seven years they shall be prostrators; but for two years they shall communicate with the people in prayer, without [being admitted to] the Oblation ᵖ.

XII.
The Discipline to be observed with Apostates.

Let them, who having been called by grace have at first shewn their zeal, and after having thrown off their girdles again returned to their vomit (so as that some of them have even purchased a place in the army,) be prostrators ten years, after they have been hearers three years; and in all these cases let the purpose and character of their repentance be examined. But the Bishop may use some favour toward those who demonstrate their conversion in fear, and tears, and patience, and good works; in reality, as well as appearance; so as after the determined time of being hearers, to let them partake of the prayers, and determine yet more favourably respecting them. But those who hear their sentence with indifference, and think the form of their entering the Church enough for their conversion; let them fulfil their whole time.

XIII.
Of those who desire Communion at the point of Death.

Let none [of the fore-mentioned persons under penance] be deprived of the last and most necessary

---

ᵖ These several periods of penance are best explained by reference to the allotment of space in the ancient churches, which were so arranged as to mark the distinctions made between those who were or were not admitted to partake of the Lord's Table.

καὶ ἀναγκαιοτάτου ἐφοδίου μὴ ἀποστερεῖσθαι. εἰ δὲ ἀπογνωσθεὶς καὶ κοινωνίας πάλιν τυχὼν, πάλιν ἐν τοῖς ζῶσιν ἐξετασθῇ, μετὰ τῶν κοινωνούντων τῆς εὐχῆς μόνης ἔστω. καθόλου δὲ καὶ περὶ παντὸς οὑτινοσοῦν ἐξοδεύοντος αἰτοῦντος δὲ μετασχεῖν εὐχαριστίας, ὁ ἐπίσκοπος μετὰ δοκιμασίας μεταδιδότω τῆς προσφορᾶς.

ΚΑΝΩΝ ΙΔ.

Περὶ τῶν κατηχουμένων καὶ παραπεσόντων ἔδοξε τῇ ἁγίᾳ καὶ μεγάλῃ συνόδῳ, ὥστε τριῶν ἐτῶν αὐτοὺς ἀκροωμένους μόνον μετὰ ταῦτα εὔχεσθαι μετὰ τῶν κατηχρυμένων.

ΚΑΝΩΝ ΙΕ.

Διὰ τὸν πολὺν τάραχον καὶ τὰς στάσεις τὰς γινομένας, ἔδοξε παντάπασι περιαιρεθῆναι τὴν συνήθειαν τὴν παρὰ τὸν κανόνα εὑρεθεῖσαν ἔν τισι μέρεσιν· ὥστε ἀπὸ πόλεως εἰς πόλιν μὴ μεταβαίνειν, μήτε ἐπίσκοπον, μήτε πρεσβύτερον, μήτε διάκονον. εἰ δέ τις μετὰ τὸν τῆς ἁγίας καὶ μεγάλης συνόδου ὅρον, τοιούτῳ τινὶ ἐπιχειρήσειεν, ἢ ἐπιδοίη ἑαυτὸν πράγματι τοιούτῳ, ἀκυρωθήσεται ἐξάπαντος τὸ κατασκεύασμα, καὶ ἀποκατασταθήσεται τῇ ἐκκλησίᾳ, ἧς ὁ ἐπίσκοπος ἢ ὁ πρεσβύτερος ἐχειροτονήθη.

ΚΑΝΩΝ Ι϶.

Ὅσοι ῥιψοκινδύνως μήτε τὸν φόβον τοῦ Θεοῦ πρὸ ὀφθαλμῶν ἔχοντες, μήτε τὸν ἐκκλησιαστικὸν κανόνα εἰδότες ἀναχω-

Viaticum ⁹ when he departs out of this life; but the Old Canonical Law shall be observed: but if such a person being given over for dead, and thereupon do again recover, let him remain among them who communicate, in prayers only. Let the Bishop, upon examination, impart of the offering to all who desire to partake of the Eucharist, at the hour of death.

XIV.
OF LAPSED CATECHUMENS.

It seems good to the holy and great Synod, that catechumens having lapsed, shall be hearers only for three years; and afterwards pray with the catechumens ʳ.

XV.
CLERGY MUST KEEP TO THEIR OWN PARISHES.

For the taking away the custom which prevails in some places contrary to Canon, it is decreed, on account of disturbances and disputes that have occurred, that neither Bishop, Priest, nor Deacon, remove from city to city ˢ; and that if any one after the decree of the holy and great Synod attempt it, all the proceedings in this case shall be null, and the party shall be restored to the Church in which he was ordained.

XVI.
OF THE BISHOP'S JURISDICTION IN HIS DIOCESE.

No Priest, Deacon, nor any belonging to the clergy, ought to be received in another Church, if, having

---

⁹ The "provision for his journey;" the reception of Christ's Body and Blood, was, by the "old Canonical Law"—older, that is, than the fourth century—permitted to all who would embrace this means of reconciliation.

ʳ There were four classes of catechumens. See Bingham, x. 2.

ˢ Canon Apostol. xiv.

ρήσουσι τῆς ἐκκλησίας, πρεσβύτεροι ἢ διάκονοι, ἢ ὅλως ἐν τῷ κανόνι ἐξεταζόμενοι· οὗτοι οὐδαμῶς δεκτοὶ ὀφείλουσιν εἶναι ἐν ἑτέρᾳ ἐκκλησίᾳ, ἀλλὰ πᾶσαν αὐτοῖς ἀνάγκην ἐπάγεσθαι χρὴ, ἀναστρέφειν εἰς τὰς ἑαυτῶν παροικίας, ἢ ἐπιμένοντας, ἀκοινωνήτους εἶναι προσήκει. εἰ δὲ καὶ τολμήσειέν τις ὑφαρπάσαι τὸν τῷ ἑτέρῳ διαφέροντα, καὶ χειροτονῆσαι ἐν τῇ αὐτοῦ ἐκκλησίᾳ, μὴ συγκατατιθεμένου τοῦ ἰδίου ἐπισκόπου, οὗ ἀνεχώρησεν ὁ ἐν τῷ κανόνι ἐξεταζόμενος, ἄκυρος ἔστω ἡ χειροτονία.

ΚΑΝΩΝ ΙΖ.

Ἐπειδὴ πολλοὶ ἐν τῷ κανόνι ἐξεταζόμενοι τὴν πλεονεξίαν καὶ τὴν αἰσχροκερδίαν διώκοντες, ἐπελάθοντο τοῦ θείου γράμματος λέγοντος, τὸ ἀργύριον αὐτοῦ οὐκ ἔδωκεν ἐπὶ τόκῳ, καὶ δανείζοντες, ἑκατοστὰς ἀπαιτοῦσιν· ἐδικαίωσεν ἡ ἁγία καὶ μεγάλη σύνοδος, ὡς εἴ τις εὑρεθείη μετὰ τὸν ὅρον τοῦτον τόκους λαμβάνειν, ἐκ μεταχειρήσεως ἢ ἄλλως μετερχόμενος τὸ πρᾶγμα, ἢ ἡμιολίας ἀπαιτῶν, ἢ ὅλως ἕτερόν τι ἐπινοῶν αἰσχροῦ κέρδους ἕνεκα, καθαιρεθήσεται τοῦ κλήρου, καὶ ἀλλότριος τοῦ κανόνος ἔσται.

ΚΑΝΩΝ ΙΗ.

Ἦλθεν εἰς τὴν ἁγίαν καὶ μεγάλην σύνοδον, ὅτι ἔν τισι τόποις καὶ πόλεσι, τοῖς πρεσβυτέροις τὴν εὐχαριστίαν οἱ διάκονοι διδόασιν, ὥσπερ οὔτε ὁ κανὼν οὔτε ἡ συνήθεια παρέδωκε, τοὺς ἐξουσίας μὴ ἔχοντας προσφέρειν, τοῖς προσφέρουσι διδόναι τὸ σῶμα τοῦ Χριστοῦ. κἀκεῖνο δὲ ἐγνωρίσθη, ὅτι ἤδη τινὲς τῶν διακόνων καὶ πρὸ τῶν ἐπισκόπων τῆς εὐχαριστίας ἅπτονται. ταῦτα οὖν πάντα περιῃρήσθω· καὶ ἐμμενέτωσαν οἱ διάκονοι τοῖς ἰδίοις μέτροις, εἰδότες ὅτι τοῦ μὲν ἐπισκόπου ὑπηρέται εἰσὶν, τῶν δὲ πρεσβυτέρων ἐλάττους τυγχάνουσι.

left their own Church, they go thither inconsiderately, without the fear of God, and regard to the Canon of the Church; but must be compelled to return to their proper parishes, or, if they do not, be excommunicated[t]: and if any one dare surreptitiously to ordain him in his own church who belongs to another, without the consent of his Bishop, let the ordination be null.

XVII.
Usury forbidden to the Clergy.

BECAUSE many of the Ecclesiastical order being led away by covetousness and a desire of base gain, have forgotten the Holy Scripture, which saith "He gave not his money on usury," do exercise usury, so as to demand every month the hundredth part of the principal[u], the holy Synod thinks it just, that if any take [such] use, by secret transaction, or by demanding the principal, and one-half of the principal for interest, or contrive any other fraud for filthy lucre's sake, let him be deposed from the clergy, and struck out of the list.

XVIII.
Of the Privileges of Priests.

IT has come to the knowledge of the holy and great Synod, that Deacons, who have not power to make the Offering, administer the Body of Christ to Priests who have that power, which neither Canon nor custom permits. It has also been made known that Deacons touch the Eucharist even before Bishops. Let all such

---

[t] Or suspended.
[u] 12 per cent., the legal rate of usury. See *Corpus Juris Civilis;* Codex IV., xxxii. 26, xxxiii. 2; Digest XXII. ii. 4.

λαμβανέτωσαν δὲ κατὰ τὴν τάξιν τὴν εὐχαριστίαν μετὰ τοὺς πρεσβυτέρους, ἢ τοῦ ἐπισκόπου διδόντος αὐτοῖς, ἢ τοῦ πρεσβυτέρου· ἀλλὰ μηδὲ καθῆσθαι ἐν μέσῳ τῶν πρεσβυτέρων ἐξέστω τοῖς διακόνοις· παρὰ κανόνα γὰρ καὶ παρὰ τάξιν ἐστὶ τὸ γινόμενον. εἰ δέ τις μὴ θέλοι πειθαρχεῖν καὶ μετὰ τούτους τοὺς ὅρους, πεπαύσθω τῆς διακονίας.

ΚΑΝΩΝ ΙΘ.

Περὶ τῶν Παυλιανισάντων, εἶτα προσφυγόντων τῇ καθολικῇ ἐκκλησίᾳ, ὅρος ἐκτέθειται ἀναβαπτίζεσθαι αὐτοὺς ἐξάπαντος. εἰ δέ τινες ἐν τῷ παρεληλυθότι χρόνῳ ἐν τῷ κλήρῳ ἐξητάσθησαν, εἰ μὲν ἄμεμπτοι καὶ ἀνεπίληπτοι φανεῖεν, ἀναβαπτισθέντες χειροτονείσθωσαν ὑπὸ τοῦ τῆς καθολικῆς ἐκκλησίας ἐπισκόπου. εἰ δὲ ἡ ἀνάκρισις ἀνεπιτηδείους αὐτοὺς εὑρίσκοι, καθαιρεῖσθαι αὐτοὺς προσήκει. ὡσαύτως δὲ καὶ περὶ τῶν διακονισσῶν, καὶ ὅλως περὶ τῶν ἐν τῷ κανόνι ἐξεταζομένων ὁ αὐτὸς τύπος παραφυλαχθήσεται. ἐμνήσθημεν δὲ τῶν διακονισσῶν τῶν ἐν τῷ σχήματι ἐξετασθεισῶν, ἐπεὶ μηδὲ χειροθεσίαν τινὰ ἔχουσι, ὥστε ἐξάπαντος ἐν τοῖς λαϊκοῖς α᾿τὰς ἐξετάζεσθαι.

ΚΑΝΩΝ Κ.

Ἐπειδή τινές εἰσιν ἐν τῇ κυριακῇ γόνυ κλίνοντες, καὶ ἐν ταῖς τῆς πεντηκοστῆς ἡμέραις, ὑπὲρ τοῦ πάντα ἐν πάσῃ παροικίᾳ ὁμοίως παραφυλάττεσθαι, ἑστῶτας ἔδοξε τῇ ἁγίᾳ συνόδῳ τὰς εὐχὰς ἀποδιδόναι τῷ Θεῷ.

practices therefore be done away, and let the Deacons keep within their proper bounds, and receive the Eucharist either from the Bishop, whose attendants they are, or from the Priests, whose inferiors they are. Let not the Deacons sit among the Priests contrary to Canon and order: and if any will not obey, let him desist from the function of a Deacon [v].

XIX.
Certain Schismatics to be Re-baptized.

A decree has been made, that Paulianists[x] returning to the Catholic Church be re-baptized; and that they, who were of their clergy, if they be under no blemish, be re-baptized and ordained by the Bishop of the Catholic Church; but if upon examination they do not appear to be qualified, let them be deposed. The same rule shall apply to their Deaconesses[y], and to all of the clerical order; but those who are Deaconesses in habit only, having received no imposition of hands, we ruled should be treated as laity.

XX.
On Kneeling at Certain Seasons.

Because there are some who kneel on the Lord's Day, and even in the days of Pentecost[z]; that all things may be uniformly performed in every parish, it seems good to the holy Synod, that prayers be made to God standing.

---

[v] For an account of the duties of Deacons see Bingham, ii. 20.
[x] These heretics did not baptize into the name of the Father, Son, and Holy Ghost. (St. Matt. xxviii. 19). See Can. Apost. 50.
[y] See Bingham, ii. 22: Can. Chalc. xv. note.
[z] That is, the fifty days from Easter to Whitsun-Day. See Tert. de cor. Mil. 3, 4.

CANONES
CONCILII CONSTANTINOPOLITANI GENERALIS.
A.D. 381.

Κανόνες τῶν ἑκατὸν πεντήκοντα ἁγίων πατέρων τῶν ἐν Κωνσταντινουπόλει συνελθόντων.

Epistola Synodi ad Theodosium Magnum.

Προσφωνητικὸς τῆς αὐτῆς ἁγίας συνόδου πρὸς τὸν εὐλαβέστατον βασιλέα Θεοδόσιον τὸν μέγαν, ᾧ ὑπέταξαν τοὺς παρ' αὐτῶν ἐκτεθέντας κανόνας.

Τῷ εὐσεβεστάτῳ βασιλεῖ Θεοδοσίῳ ἡ ἁγία σύνοδος τῶν ἐπισκόπων τῶν ἐκ διαφόρων ἐπαρχιῶν συνελθόντων ἐν Κωνσταντινουπόλει.

ΑΡΧΗ μὲν ἡμῖν τοῦ πρὸς τὴν σὴν εὐσέβειαν γράμματος, εὐχαριστία πρὸς τὸν Θεὸν τὸν ἀναδείξαντα τῆς ὑμετέρας εὐσεβείας τὴν βασιλείαν, ἐπὶ κοινῇ τῶν ἐκκλησιῶν εἰρήνῃ καὶ τῆς ὑγιοῦς πίστεως στηριγμῷ· ἀποδιδόντες δὲ τῷ Θεῷ τὴν ὀφειλομένην εὐχαριστίαν, ἀναγκαίως καὶ τὰ γεγενημένα κατὰ τὴν ἁγίαν σύνοδον πρὸς τὴν σὴν εὐσέβειαν ἀναφέρομεν· καὶ ὅτι συνελθόντες εἰς τὴν Κωνσταντινούπολιν κατὰ τὸ γράμμα τῆς σῆς εὐσεβείας, πρῶτον μὲν ἀνενεωσάμεθα τὴν πρὸς ἀλλήλους ὁμόνοιαν· ἔπειτα δὲ καὶ συντόμους ὅρους ἐξεφωνήσαμεν, τήν τε τῶν πατέρων πίστιν τῶν ἐν Νικαίᾳ κυρώσαντες, καὶ τὰς κατ' αὐτῆς ἐκφυείσας αἱρέσεις ἀναθεματίσαντες. πρὸς δὲ τούτοις, καὶ ὑπὲρ τῆς εὐταξίας τῶν ἐκκλησιῶν ῥητοὺς κανόνας ὡρίσαμεν· ἅπερ ἅπαντα τῷδε ἡμῶν τῷ γράμματι ὑπετάξαμεν. δεόμεθα τοίνυν τῆς σῆς εὐσεβείας ἐπικυρωθῆναι τῆς συνόδου

THE CONSTANTINOPOLITAN CANONS.

THE CANONS OF THE 150 HOLY FATHERS GATHERED TOGETHER AT CONSTANTINOPLE [a].

The Letter of the Synod to Theodosius the Great.

To the most religious and pious Emperor Theodosius, the holy Synod of Bishops assembled from different provinces in Constantinople.

We begin our letter to your Piety with thanksgiving to God, who has appointed the dominion of your Piety, for the common peace of the Churches, and the confirmation of the sound faith. And having rendered to God the thanksgiving which is due to Him, we, in our bounden duty, set forth to your Piety the things which have been done in the holy Synod. So then having assembled at Constantinople according to the letter of your Piety, we first renewed our agreement with one another; and then pronounced some short definitions, ratifying the faith of the Nicene Fathers, and anathematizing the heresies which have sprung up contrary to it. In addition to this, and for the right ordering of the Churches, we have established certain Canons, all which we have subjoined to this our letter. We pray therefore your Clemency, that the decree of the Synod may be confirmed, that

---

[a] These Canons were made against Macedonius, the heretical Bishop of Constantinople, who denied the divinity of the Holy Ghost. Timothy of Alexandria and others successively presided in it.

τὴν ψῆφον· ἵν' ὥσπερ τοῖς τῆς κλήσεως γράμμασί τὴν ἐκκλησίαν τετίμηκας, οὕτω καὶ τῶν δοξάντων ἐπισφραγίσῃς τὸ τέλος. ὁ δὲ Κύριος στηρίξῃ σου τὴν βασιλείαν ἐν εἰρήνῃ καὶ δικαιοσύνῃ, καὶ παραπέμψῃ γενεαῖς γενεῶν, καὶ προσθείη τῷ ἐπιγείῳ κράτει καὶ τῆς βασιλείας τῆς ἐπουρανίου τὴν ἀπόλαυσιν. ἐρρωμένον σε, καὶ ἐν πᾶσι τοῖς καλοῖς διαπρέποντα ὁ Θεὸς χαρίσαιτο τῇ οἰκουμένῃ, εὐχαῖς τῶν ἁγίων, τὸν ὡς ἀληθῶς εὐσεβέστατον καὶ θεοφιλέστατον βασιλέα.

Τάδε ὥρισαν οἱ ἐν Κωνσταντινουπόλει χάριτι Θεοῦ συνελθόντες ἐπίσκοποι ἐκ διαφόρων ἐπαρχιῶν κατὰ κλῆσιν τοῦ εὐσεβεστάτου βασιλέως Θεοδοσίου.

ΚΑΝΩΝ Α.

Μὴ ἀθετεῖσθαι τὴν πίστιν τῶν πατέρων τῶν τριακοσίων δεκαοκτὼ τῶν ἐν Νικαίᾳ τῆς Βιθυνίας συνελθόντων· ἀλλὰ μένειν ἐκείνην κυρίαν, καὶ ἀναθεματισθῆναι πᾶσαν αἵρεσιν· καὶ ἰδικῶς τὴν τῶν Εὐνομιανῶν, εἴτουν Ἀνομοίων· καὶ τὴν τῶν Ἀρειανῶν, εἴτουν Εὐδοξιανῶν· καὶ τὴν τῶν Ἡμιαρειάνων εἴτουν Πνευματομάχων· καὶ τὴν τῶν Σαβελλιανῶν, καὶ τὴν τῶν Μαρκελλιανῶν, καὶ τὴν τῶν Φωτεινιανῶν, καὶ τὴν τῶν Ἀπολλιναριστῶν.

as you have honoured the Church by the letters of citation, so also you may set your seal to the conclusion of what has been decreed. May the Lord establish your dominion in peace and righteousness, and prolong it from generation to generation, and add unto the earthly dominion the enjoyment also of the heavenly kingdom. May God grant unto the world, by the prayers of the Saints, that you may be in health and wealth and eminent in all good things, as being a most truly religious and most pious Emperor.

These things the Bishops, who having been cited by the most religious Emperor Theodosius, were assembled at Constantinople from their several provinces, decreed and ordered.

I.

THE NICENE CREED TO BE RETAINED.

THE Creed of the three hundred and eighteen Bishops assembled at Nice shall not be made void, but remain firm; and every heresy [b] be anathematized, especially that of the Eunomians, and Eudoxians, the Semi-Arians, or Pneumato-machi, those of the Sabellians, Marcellians, Photinians, Apollinarians.

---

[b] The followers of Eunomius and Eudoxius were Anomæans or rigid Arians. The Semi-Arians or Homoiousians, and Pneumatomachi maintained that the Second and Third Persons of the Blessed Trinity were created. The Sabellians or Patripassians denied the Personality of the Son and the Holy Spirit. Against the Marcellian heresy, which was founded on 1 Cor. xv. 24—28, the addition "of whose kingdom there shall be no end" was made to the Nicene Creed. The Photinians, besides their agreement with the Sabellians, asserted that Christ was a mere man. The Apollinarians denied the existence of the "reasonable soul" in the perfect humanity of Christ.

ΚΑΝΩΝ Β.

Τοὺς ὑπὲρ διοίκησιν ἐπισκόπους, ταῖς ὑπερορίοις ἐκκλησίαις μὴ ἐπιέναι, μηδὲ συγχέειν τὰς ἐκκλησίας· ἀλλὰ κατὰ τοὺς κανόνας, τὸν μὲν Ἀλεξανδρείας ἐπίσκοπον, τὰ ἐν Αἰγύπτῳ μόνον οἰκονομεῖν· τοὺς δὲ τῆς ἀνατολῆς ἐπισκόπους, τὴν ἀνατολὴν μόνην διοικεῖν· φυλαττομένων τῶν ἐν τοῖς κανόσι τοῖς κατὰ Νικαίαν πρεσβείων τῇ Ἀντιοχέων ἐκκλησίᾳ· καὶ τοὺς τῆς Ἀσιανῆς διοικήσεως ἐπισκόπους τὰ κατὰ τὴν Ἀσιανὴν μόνον οἰκονομεῖν· καὶ τοὺς τῆς Ποντικῆς, τὰ τῆς Ποντικῆς μόνα· καὶ τοὺς τῆς Θρᾳκικῆς, τὰ τῆς Θρᾳκικῆς μόνον οἰκονομεῖν. ἀκλήτους δὲ ἐπισκόπους ὑπὲρ διοίκησιν μὴ ἐπιβαίνειν ἐπὶ χειροτονίᾳ ἤ τισιν ἄλλαις οἰκονομίαις ἐκκλησιαστικαῖς· φυλαττομένου δὲ τοῦ προγεγραμμένου περὶ τῶν διοικήσεων κανόνος, εὔδηλον ὡς τὰ καθ᾽ ἑκάστην ἐπαρχίαν ἡ τῆς ἐπαρχίας σύνοδος διοικήσει κατὰ τὰ ἐν Νικαίᾳ ὡρισμένα. τὰς δὲ ἐν τοῖς βαρβαρικοῖς ἔθνεσι τοῦ Θεοῦ ἐκκλησίας, οἰκονομεῖσθαι χρὴ κατὰ τὴν κρατήσασαν συνήθειαν τῶν πατέρων.

ΚΑΝΩΝ Γ.

Τὸν μέν τοι Κωνσταντινουπόλεως ἐπίσκοπον ἔχειν τὰ πρεσβεῖα τῆς τιμῆς μετὰ τὸν τῆς Ῥώμης ἐπίσκοπον, διὰ τὸ εἶναι αὐτὴν νέαν Ῥώμην.

ΚΑΝΩΝ Δ.

Περὶ Μαξίμου τοῦ κυνικοῦ καὶ τῆς κατ᾽ αὐτὸν ἀταξίας τῆς ἐν Κωνσταντινουπόλει γενομένης, ὥστε μήτε τὸν Μάξιμον

II.
BISHOPS ARE TO KEEP TO THEIR OWN DIOCESES.

LET not Bishops go out of their diocese to churches out of their bounds, nor bring confusion on the Churches; but let the Bishop of Alexandria, according to the Canon, administer the affairs of Egypt, and the Bishops of the East the affairs of the East only, with a salvo to the ancient privileges of the Church of Antioch, mentioned in the Nicene Canons. Let the Bishops of the Asian diocese administer the Asian affairs only; and they of Pontus the Pontic, and they of Thrace the Thracian; and let not Bishops go out of their dioceses to ordinations, or any other administrations, unless they be invited. And the aforesaid Canon concerning dioceses being observed, it is evident that the provincial Synod will have the management of every province, as was decreed at Nice. The churches of God amongst the barbarians must be governed according to the customs which prevailed with their ancestors.

III.
THE PRECEDENCE OF ROME AND CONSTANTINOPLE.

THAT the Bishop of Constantinople have the prerogative of honour next after the Bishop of Rome[e]: for Constantinople is New Rome.

IV.
OF CERTAIN IRREGULARITIES AT CONSTANTINOPLE.

CONCERNING Maximus[d] the Cynic and the disorder which took place at Constantinople on his account, it

[e] See *Corpus Juris Civilis*, Nouell. 131. 2; S. Iren. adv. Hær., iii. 3.

[d] He was irregularly elected and ordained by certain Egyptian Bishops. It is to be noted that it is his Jurisdiction, and not his Orders, that is annulled.

ἐπίσκοπον ἢ γενέσθαι ἢ εἶναι, μήτε τοὺς παρ' αὐτοῦ χειροτονηθέντας ἐν οἱῳδήποτε βαθμῷ κλήρου πάντων καὶ τῶν περὶ αὐτὸν καὶ τῶν παρ' αὐτοῦ γενομένων ἀκυρωθέντων.

ΚΑΝΩΝ Ε.

Περὶ τοῦ τόμου τῶν δυτικῶν· καὶ τοὺς ἐν Ἀντιοχείᾳ ἀπεδεξάμεθα τοὺς μίαν ὁμολογοῦντας Πατρὸς, καὶ Υἱοῦ, καὶ ἁγίου Πνεύματος θεότητα.

ΚΑΝΩΝ ς.

Ἐπειδὴ πολλοὶ τὴν ἐκκλησιαστικὴν εὐταξίαν συγχεῖν καὶ ἀνατρέπειν βουλόμενοι, φιλέχθρως καὶ συκοφαντικῶς αἰτίας τινὰς κατὰ τῶν οἰκονομούντων τὰς ἐκκλησίας ὀρθοδόξων ἐπισκόπων συμπλάσσουσιν, οὐδὲν ἕτερον ἢ χραίνειν τὰς τῶν ἱερέων ὑπολήψεις καὶ ταραχὰς τῶν εἰρηνευόντων λαῶν κατασκευάζειν ἐπιχειροῦντες· τούτου ἕνεκεν ἤρεσεν τῇ ἁγίᾳ συνόδῳ τῶν ἐν Κωνσταντινουπόλει συνεδραμόντων ἐπισκόπων, μὴ ἀνεξετάστως προσίεσθαι τοὺς κατηγόρους, μηδὲ πᾶσιν ἐπιτρέπειν τὰς κατηγορίας ποιεῖσθαι κατὰ τῶν οἰκονομούντων τὰς ἐκκλησίας, μηδὲ μὴν πάντας ἀποκλείειν. ἀλλ' εἰ μέν τις οἰκείαν τινὰ μέμψιν, τοῦτ' ἔστιν, ἰδιωτικὴν, ἐπαγάγοι τῷ ἐπισκόπῳ, ὡς πλεονεκτηθεὶς, ἢ ἄλλό τι παρὰ τὸ δίκαιον παρ' αὐτοῦ πεπονθώς· ἐπὶ τῶν τοιούτων κατηγοριῶν μὴ ἐξετάζεσθαι, μήτε πρόσωπον τοῦ κατηγόρου, μήτε τὴν θρησκείαν. χρὴ γὰρ παντὶ τρόπῳ, τότε συνειδὸς τοῦ ἐπισκόπου ἐλεύθερον εἶναι, καὶ τὸν ἀδικεῖσθαι λέγοντα, οἵας ἂν ᾖ θρησκείας τῶν δικαίων τυγχάνειν. εἰ δὲ ἐκκλησιαστικὸν εἴη τὸ ἐπιφερόμενον ἔγκλημα τῷ ἐπισκόπῳ, τότε δοκιμάζεσθαι χρὴ τῶν κατηγορούντων τὰ πρόσωπα· ἵνα πρῶτον μὲν αἱρετικοῖς μὴ ἐξῇ κατηγορίας κατὰ τῶν ὀρθοδόξων ἐπισκόπων ὑπὲρ ἐκκλησιαστικῶν πραγμάτων ποιεῖσθαι. αἱρετικοὺς δὲ λέγομεν, τούς τε πάλαι τῆς ἐκκλησίας ἀποκηρυχθέντας, καὶ τοὺς μετὰ ταῦτα ὑφ' ἡμῶν ἀναθεματισθέν-

is decreed that he neither was nor is a Bishop, nor they who have been ordained by him are in any rank of the clergy; all that has been done to him, or by him, being actually null.

V.
OF THE WESTERN CONFESSION OF FAITH.

As to what concerns the tome* of the Western Bishops, we receive also those at Antioch, who acknowledge the one Deity of Father, Son, and Holy Ghost.

VI.
CONCERNING THE ACCUSERS OF ORTHODOX BISHOPS.

IF any one bring a private or personal accusation against a Bishop, as having been oppressed or injured by him, no regard shall be had of the person or religion of him who brings the accusation; but if an ecclesiastical crime be objected against the Bishop, then the person of him who brings the accusation shall be considered, that so heretics and schismatics † may not accuse orthodox Bishops; and that they of the clergy or laity who stand condemned, or deposed, or excommunicated, may not accuse a Bishop till they are cleared from the crimes charged upon them: and that likewise they who are themselves accused beforehand, be not allowed to accuse a Bishop or clergyman till

---

* The genuineness of this and the two following Canons is uncertain, as is also the subject of the Tome. Not improbably it is either the Sardican Confession of Faith, or some other that passed between Rome and Antioch a few years before the present Council.

† There were three classes of such persons,—Heretics, whose doctrine was contrary to the Catholic Faith; Schismatics, who separated from the Church on matters of discipline and minor questions of doctrine; and Maintainers of conventicles.

τας. πρὸς δὲ τούτοις, καὶ τοὺς τὴν πίστιν μὲν τὴν ὑγιῆ προσποιουμένους ὁμολογεῖν, ἀποσχίσαντας δὲ καὶ ἀντισυνάγοντας τοῖς κανονικοῖς ἡμῖν ἐπισκόποις. ἔπειτα δὲ καὶ εἴ τινες τῶν ἀπὸ τῆς ἐκκλησίας ἐπὶ αἰτίαις τισὶ προκατεγνωσμένοι εἶεν καὶ ἀποβεβλημένοι, ἢ ἀκοινώνητοι, εἴτε ἀπὸ κλήρου, εἴτε ἀπὸ λαϊκοῦ τάγματος· μηδὲ τούτοις ἐξεῖναι κατηγορεῖν ἐπισκόπου, πρὶν ἂν τὸ οἰκεῖον ἔγκλημα πρότερον ἀποδύσωνται. ὁμοίως δὲ καὶ τοὺς ὑπὸ κατηγορίαν προλαβοῦσαν ὄντας μὴ πρότερον δεκτοὺς εἰς ἐπισκόπου κατηγορίαν ἢ ἑτέρων κληρικῶν, πρὶν ἂν ἀθώους ἑαυτοὺς τῶν ἐπαχθέντων αὐτοῖς ἀποδείξωσιν ἐγκλημάτων. εἰ μέν τοι τινὲς μήτε αἱρετικοὶ, μήτε ἀκοινώνητοι εἶεν, μήτε κατεγνωσμένοι ἢ προκατηγορημένοι ἐπί τισι πλημμελήμασι, λέγοιεν δὲ ἔχειν τινὰ ἐκκλησιαστικὴν κατὰ τοῦ ἐπισκόπου κατηγορίαν· τούτους κελεύει ἡ ἁγία σύνοδος πρῶτον μὲν ἐπὶ τῶν τῆς ἐπαρχίας πάντων ἐπισκόπων ἐνίστασθαι τὰς κατηγορίας, καὶ ἐπ' αὐτῶν ἐλέγχειν τὰ ἐγκλήματα, τοῦ ἐν αἰτίαις τισὶν ἐπισκόπου. εἰ δὲ συμβαίη ἀδυνατῆσαι τοὺς ἐπαρχιώτας πρὸς διόρθωσιν τῶν ἐπιφερομένων ἐγκλημάτων τῷ ἐπισκόπῳ· τότε αὐτοὺς προσιέναι μείζονι συνόδῳ τῶν τῆς διοικήσεως ἐκείνης ἐπισκόπων, ὑπὲρ τῆς αἰτίας ταύτης συγκαλουμένων, καὶ μὴ πρότερον ἐνίστασθαι τὴν κατηγορίαν, πρὶν ἢ ἐγγράφως αὐτοὺς τὸν ἴσον αὐτοῖς ὑποτιμήσασθαι κίνδυνον, εἴπερ ἐν τῇ τῶν πραγμάτων ἐξετάσει συκοφαντοῦντες τὸν κατηγορούμενον ἐπίσκοπον ἐλεγχθεῖεν. εἰ δέ τις καταφρονήσας τῶν κατὰ τὰ προδηλωθέντα δεδογμένων, τολμήσειεν ἢ βασιλικὰς ἐνοχλεῖν ἀκοὰς, ἢ κοσμικῶν ἀρχόντων δικαστήρια, ἢ οἰκουμενικὴν σύνοδον ταράσσειν, πάντας ἀτιμάσας τοὺς τῆς διοικήσεως ἐπισκόπους· τὸν τοιοῦτον τὸ παράπαν εἰς κατηγορίαν μὴ εἶναι δεκτὸν, ὡς καθυβρίσαντα τοὺς κανόνας, καὶ τὴν ἐκκλησιαστικὴν λυμηνάμενον εὐταξίαν.

ΚΑΝΩΝ Ζ.

Τοὺς προστιθεμένους τῇ ὀρθοδοξίᾳ καὶ τῇ μερίδι τῶν σωζομένων ἀπὸ αἱρετικῶν δεχόμεθα κατὰ τὴν ὑποτεταγμένην ἀπο-

they have proved themselves to be innocent. An information against a Bishop must first be preferred before the provincial Bishops, and if they be not sufficient to rectify matters, then let it be brought before the great Synod of the diocese; and let not the informers be permitted to produce their allegations till they have obliged themselves in writing to some penalty equal [to what the Bishop, in case he be convicted, shall incur], if it be made appear that the information against the Bishop was false, and feigned: but if any one dare trouble the Emperor's ears, or the temporal judicatures, or a general council, neglecting the Bishops of the diocese, he shall by no means be allowed to give information, as being one that throws contempt and reproach upon the Canons, and subverts the ecclesiastical order.

VII.

Of the Admission of Heretics [g].

We receive Arians, Macedonians, Sabbathians, and Novatians, who call themselves Puritans, and Continents, and Quarto-decimans, or Tetradites, and Apollinarians, if from being heretics they come over to the orthodox faith, and to the party of the saved [h], giving in a written renunciation of their errors, and anathematizing every heresy, by sealing them with the sacred

[g] Besides those noticed above, the followers of Sabbatius adopted the Novatian heresy, but not until eight years after this Council; of which, therefore, this Canon cannot be an Act. The Aristeri were probably an aggravated form of the Cathari. The Quarto-decimans observed the Easter Festival with the Jews. The Montanists are another sect, of whom Tertullian was a member; they were afterwards called Phryges and Cataphryges, and finally adopted Sabellianism.

[h] That is, *The Catholic Church.* See Acts ii. ult., and 1 Cor. i. 18; E$_i$ h. ii. 8.

λουθίαν καὶ συνήθειαν. Ἀρειανοὺς μὲν καὶ Μακεδονιανοὺς καὶ Σαββατιανοὺς καὶ Νουατιανοὺς τοὺς λέγοντας ἑαυτοὺς καθαροὺς καὶ ἀριστεροὺς, (scribitur καὶ ἀρίστους) καὶ τοὺς Τεσσαρεσκαιδεκατίτας εἴτουν Τετραδίτας, καὶ Ἀπολλιναριστὰς δεχόμεθα διδόντας λιβέλλους, καὶ ἀναθεματίζοντας πᾶσαν αἵρεσιν, μὴ φρονοῦσαν ὡς φρονεῖ ἡ ἁγία τοῦ Θεοῦ καθολικὴ καὶ ἀποστολικὴ ἐκκλησία· καὶ σφραγιζομένους ἤτοι χριομένους πρῶτον τῷ ἁγίῳ μύρῳ, τό τε μέτωπον καὶ τοὺς ὀφθαλμοὺς καὶ τὰς ῥῖνας καὶ τὸ στόμα καὶ τὰ ὦτα. καὶ σφραγίζοντες αὐτοὺς, λέγομεν· σφραγὶς δωρεᾶς Πνεύματος ἁγίου. Εὐνομιανοὺς μέν τοι τοὺς εἰς μίαν κατάδυσιν βαπτιζομένους καὶ Μοντανιστὰς τοὺς ἐνταῦθα λεγομένους Φρύγας, καὶ Σαβελλιανοὺς τοὺς υἱοπατορίαν διδάσκοντας, καὶ ἕτερά τινα χαλεπὰ ποιοῦντας· καὶ τὰς ἄλλας πάσας αἱρέσεις (ἐπειδὴ πολλοί εἰσιν ἐνταῦθα, μάλιστα οἱ ἀπὸ τῆς Γαλατῶν χώρας ἐρχόμενοι)· πάντας τοὺς ἀπ' αὐτῶν θέλοντας προστίθεσθαι τῇ ὀρθοδοξίᾳ ὡς Ἕλληνας δεχόμεθα, καὶ τὴν πρώτην ἡμέραν ποιοῦμεν αὐτοὺς Χριστιανοὺς, τὴν δὲ δευτέραν κατηχουμένους, εἶτα τὴν τρίτην· ἐξορκίζομεν αὐτοὺς μετὰ τοῦ ἐμφυσᾶν τρίτον εἰς τὸ πρόσωπον καὶ εἰς τὰ ὦτα αὐτῶν. καὶ οὕτως κατηχοῦμεν αὐτοὺς, καὶ ποιοῦμεν αὐτοὺς χρονίζειν εἰς τὴν ἐκκλησίαν, καὶ ἀκροᾶσθαι τῶν γραφῶν· καὶ τότε αὐτοὺς βαπτίζομεν.

unction on the forehead, the eyes, the nostrils, the mouth, and the ears, and saying, " The seal of the gift of the Holy Spirit." The Eunomians, who are baptized with only one immersion, the Montanists, or Phrygians, and Sabellians, we receive as we do Pagans, viz. the first day we make them Christians[1], the second catechumens, the third day we exorcise them by breathing thrice into their face and ears, and make them continue a good while in the Church and hear the Scriptures, and afterwards we baptize them.

[1] That is, acknowledge them as converted; as Christians in will though not in fact.

SYMBOLUM CONSTANTINOPOL.
AD EXEMPLAR, QUOD EXTAT IN ACTIS CHALCEDONENSIS CONCILII.

ΠΙΣΤΕΥΟΜΕΝ εἰς ἕνα Θεὸν, Πατέρα παντοκράτορα, ποιητὴν οὐρανοῦ καὶ γῆς, ὁρατῶν τε πάντων καὶ ἀοράτων. Καὶ εἰς ἕνα Κύριον Ἰησοῦν Χριστὸν, τὸν Υἱὸν τοῦ Θεοῦ τὸν μονογενῆ, τὸν ἐκ τοῦ Πατρὸς γεννηθέντα πρὸ πάντων τῶν αἰώνων· φῶς ἐκ φωτὸς, Θεὸν ἀληθινὸν ἐκ Θεοῦ ἀληθινοῦ· γεννηθέντα, οὐ ποιηθέντα, ὁμοούσιον τῷ Πατρί· δι' οὗ τὰ πάντα ἐγένετο, τὸν δι' ἡμᾶς τοὺς ἀνθρώπους, καὶ διὰ τὴν ἡμετέραν σωτηρίαν, κατελθόντα ἐκ τῶν οὐρανῶν, καὶ σαρκωθέντα ἐκ Πνεύματος ἁγίου, καὶ Μαρίας τῆς παρθένου, καὶ ἐνανθρωπήσαντα· σταυρωθέντα τε ὑπὲρ ἡμῶν ἐπὶ Ποντίου Πιλάτου, καὶ παθόντα, καὶ ταφέντα, καὶ ἀνιστάντα τῇ τρίτῃ ἡμέρᾳ κατὰ τὰς γραφάς· καὶ ἀνελθόντα εἰς τοὺς οὐρανοὺς, καὶ καθεζόμενον ἐκ δεξιῶν τοῦ Πατρός· καὶ πάλιν ἐρχόμενον μετὰ δόξης κρῖναι ζῶντας καὶ νεκρούς· οὗ τῆς βασιλείας οὐκ ἔσται τέλος· Καὶ εἰς τὸ Πνεῦμα τὸ ἅγιον, τὸ Κύριον, καὶ τὸ ζωοποιὸν, τὸ ἐκ τοῦ Πατρὸς ἐκπορευόμενον, τὸ σὺν Πατρὶ καὶ Υἱῷ συμπροσκυνούμενον, καὶ συνδοξαζόμενον, τὸ λαλῆσαν διὰ τῶν προφητῶν· Εἰς μίαν ἁγίαν* καθολικὴν καὶ ἀποστολικὴν ἐκκλησίαν· ὁμολογοῦμεν ἓν βάπτισμα εἰς ἄφεσιν ἁμαρτιῶν, προσδοκῶμεν ἀνάστασιν νεκρῶν, καὶ ζωὴν τοῦ μέλλοντος αἰῶνος. Ἀμήν.

* ἁγίαν. "Sanctam" apud Def. Fid. Conc. Trident. In externis autem versionibus minime constat.

THE CREED

OF THE 150 HOLY FATHERS GATHERED TOGETHER AT CONSTANTINOPLE.

WE believe in one God, the Father Almighty, Maker of heaven and earth, and of all things visible and invisible.

And in one Lord Jesus Christ, the only-begotten Son of God, Begotten of ~~the~~ Father before all worlds, ~~God of God,~~ Light of Light, very God of very God, Begotten, not made, ~~being~~ of one substance with the Father. By Whom all things were made, Who for us men, and for our salvation came down from heaven, and was incarnate by the Holy Ghost of the Virgin Mary, and was made man, and was crucified also for us under Pontius Pilate. He suffered and was buried, and the third day He rose again according to the Scriptures, and ascended into heaven, and sitteth on the right hand of the Father: and He shall come again with glory to judge both the quick and the dead: Whose kingdom shall have no end.

And in the Holy Ghost, The Lord; and The Giver of life, Who proceedeth from the Father, Who with the Father and the Son together is worshipped and glorified, Who spake by the Prophets.

In One Holy Catholick and Apostolick Church: we acknowledge one Baptism for the remission of sins, we look for the Resurrection of the dead, and the life of the world to come. Amen.

CANONES
CONCILII EPHESINI GENERALIS.
A.D. 431.

Κάνονες τῶν διακοσίων ἁγίων καὶ μακαρίων πατέρων τῶν ἐν Ἐφέσῳ συνελθόντων.

Epistola Synodica.

Ἡ ἁγία καὶ οἰκουμενικὴ σύνοδος ἡ ἐν Ἐφέσῳ συγκροτηθεῖσα ἐκ θεσπίσματος τῶν εὐσεβεστάτων βασιλέων (Impp. Theodosii et Valentiniani), τοῖς καθ' ἑκάστην ἐπαρχίαν τε καὶ πόλιν ἐπισκόποις πρεσβυτέροις διακόνοις καὶ παντὶ τῷ λαῷ.

ΣΥΝΑΧΘΕΝΤΩΝ ἡμῶν κατὰ τὸ εὐσεβὲς γράμμα ἐν τῇ Ἐφεσίων μητροπόλει, ἀπέστησάν τινες ἐξ ἡμῶν, ὄντες τὸν ἀριθμὸν τριάκοντα μικρῷ πρός, ἔξαρχον τῆς ἑαυτῶν ἀποστασίας ἐσχηκότες τὸν τῆς Ἀντιοχέων ἐπίσκοπον Ἰωάννην· ὧν καὶ τὰ ὀνόματά ἐστι ταῦτα. πρῶτος οὗτος Ἰωάννης ὁ Ἀντιοχείας τῆς Συρίας, καὶ Ἰωάννης Δαμασκοῦ, Ἀλέξανδρος Ἀπαμείας, Ἀλέξανδρος Ἱεραπόλεως, Ἱμέριος Νικομηδείας, Φριτιλᾶς Ἡρακλείας, Ἑλλάδιος Ταρσοῦ, Μαξιμῖνος Ἀναζάρβου, Θεόδωρος Μαρκιανουπόλεως, Πέτρος Τραϊανουπόλεως, Παῦλος Ἐμίσης, Πολυχρόνιος Ἡρακλειωτῶν πόλεως, Εὐθύριος Τυάνων, Μελέτιος Νεοκαισαρείας, Θεοδώρητος Κύρου, Ἀπρίγγιος Καλχηδόνος, Μακάριος Λαοδικείας τῆς μεγάλης, Ζῶσυς Ἐσβοῦντος, Σαλούστιος Κωρύκου Κιλικίας, Ἡσύχιος Κασταβάλης Κιλικίας, Οὐαλεντῖνος Μουτλοβλάκης, Εὐστάθιος Παρνασοῦ, Φίλιππος Θεοδοσιανῶν, Δανιήλ τε, καὶ Δεξιανός, Ἰουλιανός τε, καὶ Κύριλλος, Ὀλύμπιός τε, καὶ Διογένης, Παλιός, Θεοφάνης Φιλα-

THE EPHESINE CANONS.

THE CANONS OF THE 200 HOLY AND BLESSED FATHERS GATHERED TOGETHER AT EPHESUS[*].

The Letter of the Synod.

THE holy and Œcumenical Synod which was assembled at Ephesus by the decree of our most religious Sovereign, to the Bishops, Presbyters, and Deacons, and all the people, in every Province.

WHEN we were assembled in the Metropolis of Ephesus, according to the religious decrees of the Emperors, certain persons, a little more than thirty in number, separated from us, having for the leader of their schism, John, Bishop of Antioch, whose names are as follows. First, the said John, Bishop of Antioch in Syria, John, Bishop of Damascus, Alexander of Apamæa, Alexander of Hierapolis, Himerius of Nicomedia, Fritilas of Heraclea, Helladius of Tarsus, Maximin of Anazarbus, Dorotheus of Marcianopolis, Paul of Emissa, Polychronius of Heracleopolis, Euthyrius of the Tyanensians, Meletius of Neocæsarea, Theodoret of Cyrus, Apringius of Chalcedon, (al. Chalcis,) Macarius of Laodicæa Magna, Zosys of Esbuns, Sallustius of Corycus in Cilicia, Hesychius of Castabala in Cilicia, Valentinus of Mutoblaca, Eustathius of Parnassus, Philip of Theodosiopolis, Daniel, and Decianus, and Julian, and Cyril, and Olympius, and

[*] This Council was assembled to settle the contentions raised by Nestorius, Bishop of Constantinople.

δελφείας, Τραϊανὸς Αὐγούστης, Αὐρήλιος Εἰρηνουπόλεως, Μουσαῖος Ἀράδου, Ἑλλάδιος Πτολεμαΐδος· οἵ τινες τῆς ἐκκλησιαστικῆς κοινωνίας μηδεμίαν ἔχοντες ἄδειαν ὡς ἐξ αὐθεντίας ἱερατικῆς, εἰς τὸ δύνασθαί τινας ἐκ ταύτης βλάπτειν ἢ ὠφελεῖν, διὰ τὸ καί τινας ἐν αὐτοῖς εἶναι καθηρημένους, πρὸ πάντων μὲν τὰ Νεστορίου καὶ τὰ Κελεστίου φρονήματα ἐπιφερόμενοι σαφέστατα ἀπεδείχθησαν, ἐκ τοῦ μὴ ἑλέσθαι μεθ' ἡμῶν Νεστορίου καταψηφίσασθαι· οὕς τινας δόγματι κοινῷ ἡ ἁγία σύνοδος πάσης μὲν ἐκκλησιαστικῆς κοινωνίας ἀλλοτρίους ἐποίησε, πᾶσαν δὲ αὐτῶν ἐνέργειαν ἱερατικὴν περιεῖλε, δι' ἧς ἠδύναντο βλάπτειν ἢ ὠφελεῖν τινάς.

ΚΑΝΩΝ Α.

ΕΠΕΙΔΗ δὲ ἐχρῆν καὶ τοὺς ἀπολειφθέντας τῆς ἁγίας συνόδου, καὶ μείναντας κατὰ χώραν ἢ πόλιν διά τινα αἰτίαν ἢ ἐκκλησιαστικὴν ἢ σωματικήν, μὴ ἀγνοῆσαι τὰ περὶ αὐτῶν τετυπωμένα· γνωρίζομεν τῇ ὑμετέρᾳ ἁγιότητι καὶ ἀγάπῃ, ὅτιπερ εἴ τις μητροπολίτης τῆς ἐπαρχίας ἀποστατήσας τῆς ἁγίας καὶ οἰκουμενικῆς συνόδου, προσέθετο τῷ τῆς ἀποστασίας συνεδρίῳ, ἢ μετὰ τοῦτο προστεθείη, ἢ τὰ Κελεστίου ἐφρόνησεν ἢ φρονήσει· οὗτος κατὰ τῶν τῆς ἐπαρχίας ἐπισκόπων διαπράττεσθαί τι οὐδαμῶς δύναται, πάσης ἐκκλησιαστικῆς κοινωνίας ἐντεῦθεν ἤδη ὑπὸ τῆς συνόδου ἐκβεβλημένος καὶ ἀνενέργητος ὑπάρχων· ἀλλὰ καὶ αὐτοῖς τοῖς τῆς ἐπαρχίας ἐπισκόποις καὶ τοῖς πέριξ μητροπολίταις τοῖς τὰ τῆς ὀρθοδοξίας φρονοῦσιν ὑποκείσεται εἰς τὸ πάντῃ καὶ τοῦ βαθμοῦ τῆς ἐπισκοπῆς ἐκβληθῆναι.

Diogenes, and Palladius, Theophanes of Philadelphia, Tatian of Augusta, Aurelius of Irenopolis, Musæus of Aradus, Helladius of Ptolemais. These having no privilege of ecclesiastical communion, nor any priestly authority wherewith to injure or benefit any one, inasmuch as some of them were already deposed, and all showed most clearly that they were favourable to the sentiments of Nestorius and Celestius, since they did not choose to join in our decree against Nestorius, were deposed by the common decree of the Holy Synod from all ecclesiastical communion, and all their priestly power taken away from them, by which they might have injured or benefited any one.

CANON I.

On Non-attendance at the Council.

SINCE it is necessary that those who for whatever cause, ecclesiastical or personal, having failed to attend the holy Synod, and remaining in their district or city, should not be ignorant of the things decreed, we notify to your holiness and charity, that if any Metropolitan making a defection from this great and general Council, has gone or shall go to the Apostatical Synod, or be of Cælestius' opinion, he is deprived of all ecclesiastical communion, and cannot exercise his office, so as to act against the Bishops of his province, being now and from henceforth entirely cast off by the Synod from all Church communion, and suspended; but shall be liable and subject to the Bishops of the province and to the neighbouring Metropolitans, who hold orthodox doctrine, and be degraded by them.

ΚΑΝΩΝ Β.

Εἰ δέ τινες ἐπαρχιῶται ἐπίσκοποι ἀπελείφθησαν τῆς ἁγίας συνόδου, καὶ τῇ ἀποστασίᾳ προσετέθησαν, ἢ προστεθῆναι πειραθεῖεν, ἢ καὶ ὑπογράψαντες τῇ Νεστορίου καθαιρέσει ἐπαλινδρόμησαν πρὸς τὸ τῆς ἀποστασίας συνέδριον· τούτους πάντῃ κατὰ τὸ δόξαν τῇ ἁγίᾳ συνόδῳ ἀλλοτρίους εἶναι τῆς ἱερωσύνης καὶ τοῦ βαθμοῦ ἐκπίπτειν.

ΚΑΝΩΝ Γ.

Εἰ δέ τινες καὶ τῶν ἐν ἑκάστῃ πόλει ἢ χώρᾳ κληρικῶν ὑπὸ Νεστορίου καὶ τῶν σὺν αὐτῷ ὄντων τῆς ἱερωσύνης ἐκωλύθησαν διὰ τὸ ὀρθῶς φρονεῖν· ἐδικαιώσαμεν καὶ τούτους τὸν ἴδιον ἀπολαβεῖν βαθμόν· κοινῶς δὲ τοὺς τῇ ὀρθοδόξῳ καὶ οἰκουμενικῇ συνόδῳ συμφρονοῦντας κληρικοὺς, κελεύομεν τοῖς ἀποστατήσασιν ἢ ἀφισταμένοις ἐπισκόποις μηδόλως ὑπακεῖσθαι, κατὰ μηδένα τρόπον·

ΚΑΝΩΝ Δ.

Εἰ δέ τινες ἀποστατήσαιεν τῶν κληρικῶν, καὶ τολμήσαιεν ἢ κατ' ἰδίαν ἢ δημοσίᾳ τὰ Νεστορίου ἢ τὰ Κελεστίου φρονῆσαι· καὶ τούτους εἶναι καθῃρημένους, ὑπὸ τῆς ἁγίας συνόδου δεδικαίωται.

ΚΑΝΩΝ Ε.

Ὅσοι δὲ ἐπὶ ἀτόποις πράξεσι κατεκρίθησαν ὑπὸ τῆς ἁγίας συνόδου ἢ ὑπὸ τῶν οἰκείων ἐπισκόπων· καὶ τούτοις ἀκανονίστως κατὰ τὴν ἐν ἅπασιν ἀδιαφορίαν αὐτοῦ ὁ Νεστόριος, καὶ οἱ

II.
ON THE SAME.

IF any provincial Bishops have made a defection to the Apostatical Synod[b], after they had subscribed to the deposition of Nestorius, the holy Synod decrees, that they be deposed from their priesthood and dignity.

III.
THE ACTS OF NESTORIUS DISALLOWED.

WE pronounce it just, that they who have been prohibited the exercise of their sacred function by Nestorius, for being orthodox, be restored; and we wholly forbid the clergy who agree with the orthodox and Œcumenical Synod to submit to the apostatizing, and separated Bishops.

IV.
NESTORIANS AND CÆLESTIANS CONDEMNED.

THE holy Synod gives it in charge, that all clergy who fall away, and either publicly or privately adhere to the opinions of Nestorius and Cœlestius[c], be deposed.

V.
THOSE RESTORED BY NESTORIUS ARE DEPOSED.

AND that all who upon this account have been condemned by the Synod, or their own Bishops, and whom Nestorius and those of his party have attempted or may attempt uncanonically, and according to his way of doing

---

[b] An assembly headed by John of Antioch, which excommunicated the Bishops of the Council. Compare Can. 12 of the Eng. Ch.

[c] Nestorius denied the Hypostatic union, and consequently the term "Mother of God," as applied to the Virgin Mother of Christ. Celestius was a disciple of Pelagius, and had followers who took part in the Antioch assembly.

τὰ αὐτοῦ φρονοῦντες, ἀποδοῖναι ἐπειράθησαν, ἢ πειραθεῖεν κοινωνίαν ἢ βαθμὸν, ἀνωφελήτους μένειν καὶ τούτους, καὶ εἶναι οὐδὲν ἧττον καθῃρημένους ἐδικαιώσαμεν.

ΚΑΝΩΝ ϛ.

Ὁμοίως δὲ καὶ εἴτινες βουληθεῖεν τὰ περὶ ἑκάστων πεπραγμένα ἐν τῇ ἁγίᾳ συνόδῳ τῇ ἐν Ἐφέσῳ οἱῳδήποτε τρόπῳ παρασαλεύειν· ἡ ἁγία σύνοδος ὥρισεν, εἰ μὲν ἐπίσκοποι εἶεν ἢ κληρικοὶ τοῦ οἰκείου παντελῶς ἀποπίπτειν βαθμοῦ· εἰ δὲ λαϊκοὶ, ἀκοινωνήτους ὑπάρχειν.

ΔΙΑΛΑΛΙΑ τῆς αὐτῆς ἁγίας συνόδου, ἐκφωνηθεῖσα μετὰ τὸ ἀναγνωσθῆναι τὴν ἔκθεσιν τῶν τριακοσίων δέκα καὶ ὀκτὼ ἁγίων καὶ μακαρίων πατέρων, τῶν ἐν Νικαίᾳ, καὶ τὸ δυσσεβὲς σύμβολον τὸ ὑπὸ Θεοδώρου τοῦ Μοψουεστίας πλασθὲν, καὶ ὑπὸ Χαρισίου πρεσβυτέρου Φιλαδελφίας ἐπιδοθὲν τῇ αὐτῇ κατὰ Ἔφεσον ἁγίᾳ συνόδῳ.

ΚΑΝΩΝ Ζ.

Τούτων τοίνυν ἀναγνωσθέντων, ὥρισεν ἡ ἁγία σύνοδος, ἑτέραν πίστιν μηδενὶ ἐξεῖναι προφέρειν ἤγουν συγγράφειν ἢ συντιθέναι, παρὰ τὴν ὁρισθεῖσαν παρὰ τῶν ἁγίων πατέρων τῶν ἐν τῇ Νικαέων συναχθέντων πόλει, σὺν ἁγίῳ Πνεύματι.

Τοὺς δὲ τολμῶντας ἢ συντιθέναι πίστιν ἑτέραν ἤγουν προκομίζειν ἢ προφέρειν τοῖς θέλουσιν ἐπιστρέφειν εἰς ἐπίγνωσιν τῆς ἀληθείας, ἢ ἐξ Ἑλληνισμοῦ, ἢ ἐξ Ἰουδαϊσμοῦ, ἤγουν ἐξ αἱρέσεως οἱασδήποτε· τούτους, εἰ μὲν εἶεν ἐπίσκοποι ἢ κληρικοὶ, ἀλλοτρίους εἶναι τοὺς ἐπισκόπους τῆς ἐπισκοπῆς, καὶ τοὺς κληρικοὺς τοῦ κλήρου· εἰ δὲ λαϊκοὶ εἶεν, ἀναθεματίζεσθαι.

all things indifferently, to restore them either to communion or to their rank, we think it right that they should receive no benefit, but remain excommunicated or deposed.

VI.

OBJECTORS TO THESE DECREES ARE DEPOSED.

AND that all who would set aside the acts of the holy Synod of Ephesus be deposed, if Bishops or clergymen; excommunicated, if laymen.

THE decree of the same holy Synod pronounced after the Confession of Faith of the 318 blessed Fathers of the Nicene Council had been read, as well as the impious creed made by Theodore of Mopsuçtia, and given into the same holy Synod by the priest Charisius.

VII.

THE NICENE CREED TO BE EXCLUSIVELY ADOPTED.

THESE things having been read, the holy Synod has determined that no person shall be allowed to bring forward, or to write, or to compose any other Creed besides that which was settled by the holy Fathers who were assembled in the city of Nicæa, with the Holy Spirit. But those who shall dare to compose any other Creed, or to exhibit or produce any such to those who wish to turn to the acknowledgment of the truth, whether from Heathenism, or Judaism, or any heresy whatsoever, if they are Bishops or clergymen, they shall be deposed, the Bishops from their episcopal office, and the clergymen from the clergy; but if they are of the laity, they shall be anathematized. In like manner, if any, whether Bishops or clergymen, shall

κατὰ τὸν ἴσον δὲ τρόπον, εἰ φωραθεῖέν τινες εἴτε ἐπίσκοποι, εἴτε κληρικοὶ, εἴτε λαϊκοὶ, ἢ φρονοῦντες, ἢ διδάσκοντες τὰ ἐν τῇ προκομισθείσῃ ἐκθέσει παρὰ Χαρισίου τοῦ πρεσβυτέρου, περὶ τῆς ἐνανθρωπήσεως τοῦ μονογενοῦς Υἱοῦ τοῦ Θεοῦ, ἤγουν τὰ πικρὰ καὶ διεστραμμένα τοῦ Νεστορίου δόγματα, ἃ καὶ ὑποτέτακται· ὑποκείσθωσαν τῇ ἀποφάσει τῆς ἁγίας ταύτης καὶ οἰκουμενικῆς συνόδου· ὥστε δηλονότι τὸν μὲν ἐπίσκοπον ἀπαλλοτριοῦσθαι τῆς ἐπισκοπῆς καὶ εἶναι καθηρημένον· τὸν δὲ κληρικὸν ὁμοίως ἐκπίπτειν τοῦ κλήρου· εἰ δὲ λαϊκός τις εἴη, καὶ οὗτος ἀναθεματιζέσθω, καθὰ εἴρηται.

ΨΗΦΟΣ τῆς αὐτῆς ἁγίας συνόδου, ἐκφωνηθεῖσα ἐκ προσελεύσεως γενομένης αὐτῇ παρὰ τῶν Κυπρίων ἐπισκόπων.

ΚΑΝΩΝ Η.

Πρᾶγμα παρὰ τοὺς ἐκκλησιαστικοὺς θεσμοὺς καὶ τοὺς κανόνας τῶν ἁγίων πατέρων καινοτομούμενον καὶ τῆς πάντων ἐλευθερίας ἁπτόμενον, προσήγγειλεν ὁ θεοφιλέστατος συνεπίσκοπος Ῥηγῖνος, καὶ οἱ σὺν αὐτῷ θεοφιλέστατοι ἐπίσκοποι τῆς Κυπρίων ἐπαρχίας Ζήνων καὶ Εὐάγριος· ὅθεν ἐπειδὴ τὰ κοινὰ πάθη μείζονος δεῖται τῆς θεραπείας, ὡς καὶ μείζονα τὴν βλάβην φέροντα, καὶ μάλιστα εἰ μηδὲ ἔθος ἀρχαῖον παρηκολούθησεν, ὥστε τὸν ἐπίσκοπον τῆς Ἀντιοχέων πόλεως, τὰς ἐν Κύπρῳ ποιεῖσθαι χειροτονίας, καθὰ διὰ τῶν

be discovered either holding or teaching the things contained in the exposition which was exhibited by the Presbyter Charisius[d] concerning the incarnation of the only-begotten Son of God, or the impious and profane doctrines of Nestorius, which have been put down, they shall be subjected to the sentence of this holy and Œcumenical Synod; so that if it be a Bishop who does so, he shall be removed from his bishopric, and be deposed; and in like manner if a clergyman, he shall forfeit his clerical rank; but if he be a layman, he shall be anathematized, as has before been said.

The Judgment of the holy Synod given on the petition made to it by the Cyprian Bishops.

VIII.

BISHOPS NOT TO ORDAIN OUT OF THEIR DIOCESES.

The most beloved of God, and our fellow Bishop Rheginus[e], and Zeno and Euagrius, the most religious Bishops of the Province of Cyprus, who were with him, have declared unto us an act which has been introduced contrary to the laws of the Church, and the Canons of the holy Fathers, and which affects the liberty of all. Wherefore since evils which affect the community require more attention, inasmuch as they cause greater hurt; and especially since the Bishop of Antioch has not so much as followed an ancient

[d] An orthodox Priest of Philadelphia, who brought before the Council the new Nestorian Creed, composed either by James of Constantinople, or Theodore of Mopsuetia.

[e] Rheginus, Bishop of Constantia, Zeno of Arium, and Euagrius of Soli laid a complaint against the Bishop of Antioch, whose interference was supported by the military governor of Antioch. Among the Acts of this Council are the authorised declarations of Cyril of Alexandria respecting the Incarnation.

λιβέλλων καὶ τῶν οἰκείων φωνῶν ἐδίδαξαν οἱ εὐλαβέστατοι ἄνδρες οἱ τὴν πρόσοδον τῇ ἁγίᾳ συνόδῳ ποιησάμενοι, ἔξουσι τὸ ἀνεπηρέαστον καὶ ἀβίαστον οἱ τῶν ἁγίων ἐκκλησιῶν τῶν κατὰ τὴν Κύπρον προεστῶτες, κατὰ τοὺς κανόνας τῶν ὁσίων πατέρων καὶ τὴν ἀρχαίαν συνήθειαν, δι' ἑαυτῶν τὰς χειροτονίας τῶν εὐλαβεστάτων ἐπισκόπων ποιούμενοι. τὸ δὲ αὐτὸ καὶ ἐπὶ τῶν ἄλλων διοικήσεων καὶ τῶν ἁπανταχοῦ ἐπαρχιῶν παραφυλαχθήσεται· ὥστε μηδένα τῶν θεοφιλεστάτων ἐπισκόπων ἐπαρχίαν ἑτέραν οὐκ οὖσαν ἄνωθεν καὶ ἐξαρχῆς ὑπὸ τὴν αὐτοῦ, ἤγουν τῶν πρὸ αὐτοῦ, χεῖρα καταλαμβάνειν. ἀλλ' εἰ καί τις κατέλαβεν καὶ ὑφ' ἑαυτῷ πεποίηται βιασάμενος, ταύτην ἀποδιδόναι· ἵνα μὴ τῶν πατέρων οἱ κανόνες παραβαίνωνται, μηδὲ ἐν ἱερουργίας προσχήματι, ἐξουσίας τῦφος κοσμικῆς παρεισδύηται, μηδὲ λάθωμεν τὴν ἐλευθερίαν κατὰ μικρὸν ἀπολέσαντες, ἣν ἡμῖν ἐδωρήσατο τῷ ἰδίῳ αἵματι ὁ Κύριος ἡμῶν Ἰησοῦς Χριστός, ὁ πάντων ἀνθρώπων ἐλευθερώτης.

Ἔδοξε τοίνυν τῇ ἁγίᾳ ταύτῃ καὶ οἰκουμενικῇ συνόδῳ, σώζεσθαι ἑκάστῃ ἐπαρχίᾳ καθαρὰ καὶ ἀβίαστα τὰ αὐτῇ προσόντα δίκαια ἐξαρχῆς ἄνωθεν, κατὰ τὸ πάλαι κρατῆσαν ἔθος· ἄδειαν ἔχοντος ἑκάστου μητροπολίτου τὰ ἴσα τῶν πεπραγμένων πρὸς τὸ οἰκεῖον ἀσφαλὲς ἐκλαβεῖν. εἰ δέ τις μαχόμενον τύπον τοῖς νῦν ὡρισμένοις προκομίσοι, ἄκυρον τοῦτον εἶναι ἔδοξε τῇ ἁγίᾳ ταύτῃ καὶ οἰκουμενικῇ συνόδῳ.

custom, in performing ordinations in Cyprus, as those most religious persons who have come to the holy Synod have informed us, by writing and by word of mouth, we declare, that they who preside over the holy Churches which are in Cyprus, shall preserve without gainsaying or opposition their right of performing by themselves the ordinations of the most religious Bishops, according to the Canons of the holy Fathers, and the ancient custom. The same rule shall be observed in all the other dioceses, and in the provinces everywhere, so that none of the most religious Bishops shall invade any other province, which has not heretofore from the beginning been under the hand of himself or his predecessors. But if any one has so invaded a Province, and brought it by force under himself, he shall restore it, that the Canons of the Fathers may not be transgressed, nor the pride of secular dominion be privily introduced under the appearance of a sacred office, nor we lose by little, the freedom which our Lord Jesus Christ, the deliverer of all men, has given us by His own Blood. The holy and Œcumenical Synod has therefore decreed, that the rights which have heretofore and from the beginning belonged to each province, shall be preserved to it pure and without restraint, according to the custom which has prevailed of old. Each Metropolitan having permission to take a copy of the things now transacted for his own security. But if any one shall introduce any regulation contrary to what has been now defined, the whole holy and Œcumenical Synod has decreed that it shall be of no effect.

CANONES
CHALCEDONENSIS CONCILII GENERALIS.
A.D. 451.

Κανόνες τῶν ἑξακοσίων τριάκοντα ἁγίων καὶ μακαρίων πατέρων τῶν ἐν Χαλκηδόνι συνελθόντων.

ΚΑΝΩΝ Α.

ΤΟΥΣ παρὰ τῶν ἁγίων πατέρων καθ' ἑκάστην σύνοδον ἄχρι τοῦ νῦν ἐκτεθέντας κανόνας κρατεῖν ἐδικαιώσαμεν.

ΚΑΝΩΝ Β.

Εἴ τις ἐπίσκοπος ἐπὶ χρήμασι χειροτονίαν ποιήσαιτο, καὶ εἰς πρᾶσιν καταγάγῃ τὴν ἄπρατον χάριν, καὶ χειροτονήσῃ ἐπὶ χρήμασιν ἐπίσκοπον, ἢ χωρεπίσκοπον, ἢ πρεσβύτερον, ἢ διάκονον, ἢ ἕτερόν τινα τῶν ἐν τῷ κλήρῳ κατηριθμημένων· ἢ προβάλλοιτο ἐπὶ χρήμασιν ἢ οἰκονόμον, ἢ ἔκδικον, ἢ προσμονάριον, ἢ ὅλως τινὰ τοῦ κανόνος, δι' αἰσχροκερδίαν οἰκείαν· ὁ τοῦτο ἐπιχειρήσας ἐλεγχθεὶς, περὶ τὸν οἰκεῖον κινδυνευέτω βαθμόν· καὶ ὁ χειροτονούμενος, μηδὲν ἐκ τῆς κατ' ἐμπορίαν ὠφελείσθω χειροτονίας ἢ προβολῆς· ἀλλ' ἔστω ἀλλότριος τῆς

THE CHALCEDON CANONS.

THE CANONS OF THE 630 HOLY AND BLESSED FATHERS WHO MET AT CHALCEDON[a].

I.

THE DECREES OF FORMER COUNCILS CONFIRMED.

WE pronounce it to be fit and just, that the Canons of the holy Fathers made in every Synod[b] to this present time be in full force.

II.

ORDERS AND PREFERMENT ARE NOT TO BE BOUGHT.

If any Bishop shall ordain for money, and bring down to sale the grace which cannot be sold, and ordain for money a Bishop, or Chorepiscopus, or Presbyter, or Deacon, or any other of those that are reckoned amongst the clergy; or shall for money put forward for office a Steward[c], or Defender, or Bailiff, or any one who is on the roll of the Church, through his own sordid love of gain, let him who is convicted of having attempted this forfeit his own degree, and let him who has been ordained benefit nothing by the ordination or promotion which has been made matter of traffic, but let him have no part in the dignity or charge which he obtained for

[a] The Council was assembled by the Emperor Marcian, to determine the disputes occasioned by the doctrines of Eutyches. It was presided over by the legates of the Bishop of Rome.
[b] The Laws, including those Canons enacted by provincial Councils by which the Church was governed before, are here re-enforced by the voice of a General Council of Bishops. The Emperor Justinian afterwards gave them a civil sanction. *Novell.*, 131. 1, in which these four Councils are named. See also *Basilica* L. 1, for an imperial confirmation of the Catholic faith, and pp. 78, 9.
[c] See note on Canon XIV.

E

ἀξίας ἢ τοῦ φροντίσματος, οὕπερ ἐπὶ χρήμασιν ἔτυχεν· εἰ δέ τις καὶ μεσιτεύων φανείη τοῖς οὕτω αἰσχροῖς καὶ ἀθεμίτοις λήμμασι, καὶ οὗτος, εἰ μὲν κληρικὸς εἴη, τοῦ οἰκείου ἐκπιπτέτω βαθμοῦ· εἰ δὲ λαϊκὸς ἢ μονάζων, ἀναθεματιζέσθω.

ΚΑΝΩΝ Γ.

Ἦλθεν εἰς τὴν ἁγίαν σύνοδον, ὅτι τῶν ἐν τῷ κλήρῳ κατειλεγμένων τινὲς, διὰ αἰσχροκερδίαν, ἀλλοτρίων κτημάτων γίνονται μισθωταὶ, καὶ πράγματα κοσμικὰ ἐργολαβοῦσι, τῆς μὲν τοῦ Θεοῦ λειτουργίας καταρραθυμοῦντες, τοὺς δὲ τῶν κοσμικῶν ὑποτρέχοντες οἴκους, καὶ οὐσιῶν χειρισμοὺς ἀναδεχόμενοι διὰ φιλαργυρίαν· ὥρισε τοίνυν ἡ ἁγία καὶ μεγάλη σύνοδος, μηδένα τοῦ λοιποῦ, μὴ ἐπίσκοπον, μὴ κληρικὸν, μὴ μονάζοντα, ἢ μισθοῦσθαι κτήματα, ἢ πράγματα, ἢ ἐπεισάγειν ἑαυτὸν κοσμικαῖς διοικήσεσι· πλὴν εἰ μὴ του ἐκ νόμων καλοῖτο εἰς ἀφηλίκων ἀπαραίτητον ἐπιτροπὴν, ἢ ὁ τῆς πόλεως ἐπίσκοπος [a] ἐκκλησιαστικῶν ἐπιτρέψει φροντίζειν πραγμάτων, ἢ ὀρφανῶν καὶ χηρῶν ἀπρονοήτων, καὶ τῶν προσώπων τῶν μάλιστα τῆς ἐκκλησιαστικῆς δεομένων βοηθείας, διὰ τὸν φόβον τοῦ Κυρίου. εἰ δέ τις παραβαίνειν τὰ ὡρισμένα τοῦ λοιποῦ ἐπιχειρήσοι, ὁ τοιοῦτος ἐκκλησιαστικοῖς ὑποκείσθω ἐπιτιμίοις.

[a] In distinction from the Chorepiscopus.

money. And if any person shall appear to have been the agent* in such base and illegal payments, let him also, if he be a clergyman, be deposed from his rank; or if a layman or monk, be anathematized.

III.
CLERGY ARE NOT TO FARM OR TRADE.

It has come to the knowledge of the holy Synod, that some of those who are enrolled in the clergy, do through base love of gain become hirers of other men's possessions, and make contracts in worldly business, slightly regarding the services of God, stealing into the houses of secular persons, and undertaking the management of their property through covetousness. The great and holy Synod has therefore decreed, that no one for the future, whether Bishop, Clerk, or Monk, shall either hire possessions or undertake matters of business, or intrude himself into worldly ministrations, unless he is called by the laws to the unavoidable guardianship of minors ᶠ, or his Diocesan shall commit to him the charge of ecclesiastical business, or of orphans or widows who are not provided for, and of persons who particularly need the help of the Church, for the fear of God. But if any one for the future shall attempt to transgress what has been determined, let him be subjected to ecclesiastical penalties.

---

* The clerical agent or go-between, made use of by those who obtain preferment to the cure of souls by purchase or other bargain, to enable them to evade the law.

ᶠ Corp. Jur. Civ. Instit. i. 25; Cod. V. 62—70. This, with the IVth and XXth Canons were enacted at the suggestion of the Emperor.

ΚΑΝΩΝ Δ.

Οἱ ἀληθῶς καὶ εἰλικρινῶς τὸν μονήρη μετιόντες βίον, τῆς προσηκούσης ἀξιούσθωσαν τιμῆς. ἐπειδὴ δέ τινες τῷ μοναχικῷ κεχρημένοι πο σχήματι, τάς τε ἐκκλησίας καὶ τὰ πολιτικὰ διαταράττουσι πράγματα, περιόντες ἀδιαφόρως ἐν ταῖς πόλεσιν, οὐ μὴν ἀλλὰ καὶ μοναστήρια ἑαυτοῖς συνιστᾷν ἐπιτηδεύοντες· ἔδοξε μηδένα μὲν μηδαμοῦ οἰκοδομεῖν, μηδὲ συνιστᾷν μοναστήριον, ἢ εὐκτήριον οἶκον, παρὰ γνώμην τοῦ τῆς πόλεως ⁵ ἐπισκόπου. τοὺς δὲ καθ' ἑκάστην πόλιν καὶ χώραν μονάζοντας, ὑποτετάχθαι τῷ ἐπισκόπῳ, καὶ τὴν ἡσυχίαν ἀσπάζεσθαι, καὶ πρωσέχειν μόνῃ τῇ νηστείᾳ, καὶ τῇ προσευχῇ, ἐν οἷς τόποις ἀπετάξαντο, προσκαρτεροῦντας, μήτε δὲ ἐκκλησιαστικοῖς μήτε βιωτικοῖς παρενοχλεῖν πράγμασιν, ἢ ἐπικοινωνεῖν, καταλιμπάνοντας τὰ ἴδια μοναστήρια· εἰ μή ποτε ἄρα ἐπιτραπεῖεν διὰ χρείαν ἀναγκαίαν ὑπὸ τοῦ τῆς πόλεως ἐπισκόπου. μηδένα δὲ προσδέχεσθαι ἐν τοῖς μοναστηρίοις δοῦλον ἐπὶ τὸ μονάσαι παρὰ γνώμην τοῦ ἰδίου δεσπότου. τὸν δὲ παραβαίνοντα τοῦτον ἡμῶν τὸν ὅρον, ὡρίσαμεν ἀκοινώνητον εἶναι, ἵνα μὴ τὸ ὄνομα τοῦ Θεοῦ βλασφημῆται. τὸ μέν τοι ἐπίσκοπον τῆς πόλεως, χρὴ τὴν δέουσαν πρόνοιαν ποιεῖσθαι τῶν μοναστηρίων.

ΚΑΝΩΝ Ε.

Περὶ τῶν μεταβαινόντων ἀπὸ πόλεως εἰς πύλιν ἐπισκόπων ἢ κληρικῶν, ἔδοξε τοὺς περὶ τούτων τεθέντας κανόνας παρὰ τῶν ἁγίων πατέρων ἔχειν τὴν ἰδίαν ἰσχύν.

⁵ In distinction from the Chorepiscopus.

IV.
Concerning Monks.

Let those who truly and sincerely enter upon the monastic life be counted worthy of fitting honour. But since some, using themselves of the pretext of monasticism, throw into confusion both ecclesiastical and civil affairs, going about promiscuously the cities, and endeavouring also to establish monasteries for themselves, it is decreed, that no one shall anywhere build or establish a monastery or an oratory contrary to the will of the Diocesan. And that the monks in every city or place shall be subject to the Bishop [h], and shall embrace quiet, and attend only to fasting and prayer, continuing in the places in which they have been settled, and shall neither busy themselves in ecclesiastical or secular matters, nor take part in them, leaving their own monasteries, unless indeed they are permitted to do so for any necessary purpose by the Diocesan. And that no servant shall be received into the monasteries against the consent of his master, for the purpose of becoming a monk. But if any person transgress this our decision, we have decreed that he shall be excommunicated, that the name of God may not be blasphemed. But the Diocesan must make the needful provision for the monasteries.

V.
Clergy are to Remain in their Own Place [i].

As concerning clergymen or Bishops, that remove from one city to another, it is decreed, that the Canons made by the holy Fathers be in full force.

[h] In the Russian Church the Bishop is necessarily the head of the chief monastery in his diocese.   [i] Can. Apost. 14. Nic. 15.

ΚΑΝΩΝ ς'.

Μηδένα ἀπολελυμένως χειροτονεῖσθαι, μήτε πρεσβύτερον, μήτε διάκονον, μήτε ὅλως τινὰ τῶν ἐν τῷ ἐκκλησιαστικῷ τάγματι· εἰ μὴ ἰδικῶς ἐν ἐκκλησίᾳ πόλεως ἢ κώμης, ἢ μαρτυρίῳ, ἢ μοναστηρίῳ, ὁ χειροτονούμενος ἐπικηρύττοιτο· τοὺς δὲ ἀπολύτως χειροτονουμένους ὥρισεν ἡ ἁγία σύνοδος ἄκυρον ἔχειν τὴν τοιαύτην χειροθεσίαν, καὶ μηδαμοῦ δύνασθαι ἐνεργεῖν ἐφ' ὕβρει τοῦ χειροτονήσαντος.

ΚΑΝΩΝ Ζ.

Τοὺς ἅπαξ ἐν κλήρῳ καταλεγμένους ἢ καὶ μονάσαντας ὡρίσαμεν, μήτε ἐπὶ στρατείαν, μήτε ἐπὶ ἀξίαν κοσμικὴν ἔρχεσθαι. ἢ τοῦτο τολμῶντας, καὶ μὴ μεταμελουμένους ὥστε ἐπιστρέψαι ἐπὶ τοῦτο ὃ διὰ Θεὸν πρότερον εἵλοντο, ἀναθεματίζεσθαι.

ΚΑΝΩΝ Η.

Οἱ κληρικοὶ τῶν πτωχείων καὶ μοναστηρίων, καὶ μαρτυρίων, ὑπὸ τὴν ἐξουσίαν τῶν ἐν ἑκάστῃ πόλει ἐπισκόπων, κατὰ τὴν τῶν ἁγίων πατέρων παράδοσιν, διαμενέτωσαν. καὶ μὴ κατὰ αὐθάδειαν ἀφηνιάτωσαν τοῦ ἰδίου ἐπισκόπου. οἱ δὲ τολμῶντες ἀνατρέπειν τὴν τοιαύτην διατύπωσιν καθ' οἱονδήποτε τρόπον,

VI.
NONE TO BE ORDAINED WITHOUT A CHARGE.

No man is to be ordained at large, neither Presbyter, nor Deacon, nor indeed any one who is in the ecclesiastical order; but whoever is ordained must be appointed particularly to some charge in a church of a city, or in the country, or in a martyry[k] or monastery. But as regards those who are ordained at large, the holy Synod has determined, that such an ordination is to be held void, and cannot have any effect anywhere, to the reproach of him who ordains.

VII.
CLERGY ARE NOT TO RENOUNCE THEIR CALLING.

WE have determined that those persons who have been once enrolled amongst the clergy, or who have become monks, must not enter upon a military charge, or any worldly dignity, and that those who dare to do so, and do not repent so as to return to that state which they first chose for the sake of God, shall be anathematized.

VIII.
ALL CLERGY TO BE SUBJECT TO THE BISHOP.

LET the clergy of the poor-houses, monasteries, and martyries, remain under the authority of the Bishops in each city, according to the tradition of the holy Fathers; and let them not through self-will withdraw themselves from the rule of their own Bishop. But those who dare to overturn this Canon in any way

---

[k] Shrines or churches built over the graves of martyrs. The church in which this Council was held, is called the Martyry of the holy and victorious Martyr Euphemia.

καὶ μὴ ὑποταττόμενοι τῷ ἰδίῳ ἐπισκόπῳ· εἰ μὲν εἶεν κληρικοὶ, τοῖς τῶν κανόνων ὑποκείσθωσαν ἐπιτιμίοις· εἰ δὲ μονάζοντες ἢ λαϊκοὶ ἔστωσαν ἀκοινώνητοι.

ΚΑΝΩΝ Θ.

Εἴ τις κληρικὸς πρὸς κληρικὸν πρᾶγμα ἔχοι, μὴ ἐγκαταλιμπανέτω τὸν οἰκεῖον ἐπίσκοπον, καὶ ἐπὶ κοσμικὰ δικαστήρια κατατρεχέτω· ἀλλὰ πρότερον τὴν ὑπόθεσιν γυμναζέτω παρὰ τῷ ἰδίῳ ἐπισκόπῳ· ἤγουν γνώμῃ αὐτοῦ τοῦ ἐπισκόπου, παρ' οἷς ἂν τὰ ἀμφότερα μέρη βούλωνται τὰ τῆς δίκης συγκροτείσθω. εἰ δέ τις παρὰ ταῦτα ποιήσει, κανονικοῖς ὑποκείσθω ἐπιτιμίοις. εἰ δὲ καὶ κληρικὸς πρᾶγμα ἔχοι πρὸς τὸν ἴδιον ἐπίσκοπον ἢ πρὸς ἕτερον, παρὰ τῇ συνόδῳ τῆς ἐπαρχίας δικαζέσθω. εἰ δὲ πρὸς τὸν τῆς αὐτῆς ἐπαρχίας μητροπολίτην, ἐπίσκοπος, ἢ κληρικὸς, ἀμφισβητοίη, καταλαμβανέτω ἢ τὸν ἔξαρχον τῆς διοικήσεως, ἢ τὸν τῆς βασιλευούσης Κωνσταντινουπόλεως θρόνον, καὶ ἐπ' αὐτῷ δικαζέσθω.

ΚΑΝΩΝ Ι.

Μὴ ἐξεῖναι κληρικὸν ἐν δύο πόλεων καταλέγεσθαι ἐκκλησίαις κατὰ τὸ αὐτὸ, ἐν ᾗ τε τὴν ἀρχὴν ἐχειροτονήθη, καὶ ἐν ᾗ προσέφυγεν, ὡς μείζονι δῆθεν, διὰ δόξης κενῆς ἐπιθυμίαν. τοὺς δέ γε τοῦτο ποιοῦντας, ἀποκαθίστασθαι τῇ ἰδίᾳ ἐκκλησίᾳ, ἐν ᾗ ἐξαρχῆς ἐχειροτονήθησαν, καὶ ἐκεῖ μόνον λειτουργεῖν. εἰ

whatsoever, and submit not themselves to their own Bishop, if they be of the clergy let them undergo the canonical penalties, or if they be monks or laymen, let them be excommunicated.

IX.
Clergy are not to go to Law in the Secular Courts.

If any clergyman has a suit against another clergyman, let him not leave his own Bishop and run to the secular courts of justice [k], but let him first try the question before his own Bishop, or, with the consent of the Bishop himself, before those persons whom both parties shall choose to have the hearing of the cause. And if any person shall act contrary to these decrees, let him undergo the canonical penalties. But if a clergyman has any matter either against his own or any other Bishop, let it be decided by the Synod of the Province. But if any Bishop or clergyman has a controversy against the Metropolitan of the Province itself, let him have recourse either to the Exarch [l] of the diocese, or to the throne of the imperial city of Constantinople, and there let the cause be decided.

X.
Pluralities, honorary or otherwise, disallowed.

No clergyman may be on the list of the churches of two cities at the same time, of that in which he was first ordained, and another to which he has removed as being greater, from lust of empty honour, but those persons who act thus must be restored to the Church in which they were first ordained, and there only perform

[k] 1 Cor. vi. 1, sqq.
[l] That is, the Patriarch. *Corp. Jur. Civ.*, Nouell. 123. 22.

μέν τοι ἤδη τὶς μετετέθη ἐξ ἄλλης εἰς ἄλλην ἐκκλησίαν, μηδὲν τοῖς τῆς προτέρας ἐκκλησίας, ἤτοι τῶν ὑπ' αὐτὴν μαρτυρίων ἢ πτωχείων ἢ ξεναδοχείων ἐπικοινωνεῖν πράγμασιν. τοὺς δέ γε τολμῶντας μετὰ τὸν ὅρον τῆς μεγάλης καὶ οἰκουμενικῆς ταύτης συνόδου, πράττειν τὶ τῶν νῦν ἀπηγορευμένων, ὥρισεν ἡ ἁγία σύνοδος, ἐκπίπτειν τοῦ οἰκείου βαθμοῦ.

ΚΑΝΩΝ ΙΑ.

Πάντας τοὺς πένητας καὶ δεομένους ἐπικουρίας, μετὰ δοκιμασίας ἐπιστολίοις, εἴτουν εἰρηνικοῖς ἐκκλησιαστικοῖς μόνοις ὡρίσαμεν ὁδεύειν, καὶ, μὴ συστατικαῖς, διὰ τὸ τὰς συστατικὰς ἐπιστολὰς προσήκειν τοῖς οὖσιν ἐν ὑπολήψει μόνοις παρέχεσθαι προσώποις.

ΚΑΝΩΝ ΙΒ.

Ἦλθεν εἰς ἡμᾶς, ὥς τινες παρὰ τοὺς ἐκκλησιαστικοὺς θεσμοὺς προσδραμόντες δυναστείαις, διὰ πραγματικῶν τὴν μίαν ἐπαρχίαν εἰς δύο κατέτεμον, ὡς ἐκ τούτου δύο μητροπολίτας εἶναι ἐν τῇ αὐτῇ ἐπαρχίᾳ. ὥρισεν τοίνυν ἡ ἁγία σύνοδος, τοῦ λοιποῦ μηδὲν τοιοῦτο τολμᾶσθαι παρὰ ἐπισκόπων, ἐπεὶ τὸν τούτῳ ἐπιχειροῦντα ἐκπίπτειν τοῦ ἰδίου βαθμοῦ. ὅσαι δὲ ἤδη

divine service. But if any one has been translated [m] from one Church to another, he must not take any part in the affairs of his first Church, or of the martyries, or refuges for beggars or lodging-houses belonging to it. And the holy Synod has determined, that every one, who after the decision of this great and Œcumenical Synod, shall do any of these things which have been forbidden, shall be deposed from his station.

XI.
OF CANONICAL LETTERS.

WE decree, that they who are poor and necessitous be allowed, after approval, to travel with pacific letters [n] only, and not commendatory; for letters commendatory are only for suspected persons.

XII.
STATE INTERFERENCE IN CHURCH JURISDICTION DISALLOWED.

IT has come to our knowledge that some persons contrary to the laws of the Church, having had recourse to the secular powers, have by means of State orders [o] divided one province into two, so that there are thus two Metropolitans in one province. The holy Synod has therefore determined that for the future nothing of the sort shall be attempted by the Bishops, and that he who shall put his hand to such a thing shall be de-

---

[m] That is, removed with the consent of his former Bishop. To belong to two dioceses, or to be a member of two cathedrals at one time, is contrary to the Constitution of the Church.

[n] Letters of credence were—1. Commendatory; 2. Communicatory, or pacifical; 3. Dimissory. The third sort were given only to the clergy.

[o] That is, the rescript, or letters patent of the Emperor. The Council had specially in view the case of Eustathius of Berytus.

πόλεις διὰ γραμμάτων βασιλικῶν τῷ τῆς μητροπόλεως ἐτιμήθησαν ὀνόματι, μόνης ἀπολαυέτωσαν τῆς τιμῆς, καὶ ὁ τὴν ἐκκλησίαν αὐτῆς διοικῶν ἐπίσκοπος, δηλονότι σωζομένων τῇ κατὰ ἀλήθειαν μητροπόλει τῶν οἰκείων δικαίων.

ΚΑΝΩΝ ΙΓ.

Ξένους κληρικοὺς καὶ ἀναγνώστας ἐν ἑτέρᾳ πόλει δίχα συστατικῶν γραμμάτων τοῦ ἰδίου ἐπισκόπου μηδ' ὅλως μηδαμοῦ λειτουργεῖν.

ΚΑΝΩΝ ΙΔ.

Ἐπειδὴ ἔν τισιν ἐπαρχίαις συγκεχώρηται τοῖς ἀναγνώσταις καὶ ψάλταις γαμεῖν· ὥρισεν ἡ ἁγία σύνοδος μὴ ἐξεῖναί τινι αὐτῶν ἑτερόδοξον γυναῖκα λαμβάνειν. τοὺς δὲ ἤδη ἐκ τοιούτου γάμου παιδοποιήσαντας, εἰ μὲν ἔφθασαν βαπτίσαι τὰ ἐξ αὐτῶν τεχθέντα παρὰ τοῖς αἱρετικοῖς, προσάγειν αὐτὰ τῇ κοινωνίᾳ τῆς καθολικῆς ἐκκλησίας· μὴ βαπτισθέντα δὲ, μὴ δύνασθαι ἔτι βαπτίζειν αὐτὰ παρὰ τοῖς αἱρετικοῖς, μήτε μὴν συνάπτειν πρὸς γάμον αἱρετικῷ, ἢ Ἰουδαίῳ, ἢ Ἕλληνι, εἰ μὴ ἄρα ἐπαγγέλλοιτο μετατίθεσθαι εἰς τὴν ὀρθύδοξον πίστιν τὸ συναπτόμενον

posed from his own rank. Such cities, however, as have been already honoured with the name of Metropolis by royal letters, and the Bishop who has the charge of the Church of such a city, shall enjoy the honorary title only, the proper rights being preserved to that which is in truth the Metropolis.

XIII.
Of Letters Commendatory.

Foreign clergymen and readers shall by no means officiate at all in any other city, without letters commendatory from their own Bishop.

XIV.
Mixed Marriages of the Minor Orders [p] forbidden.

Since in some provinces it is allowed to the readers and singers to marry [q], the holy Synod has determined, that it shall not be lawful for any of them to marry a woman of heterodox opinions. But those who have already had children by such marriage, if their children have been previously baptized amongst heretics, must bring them to the communion of the Catholic Church. If, however, they have not been baptized, they may not baptize them amongst heretics, nor join them in marriage to an heretic, or Jew, or heathen, unless the person who is married to the orthodox per-

---

[p] There are nine names by which these are distinguished. Of these, the five principal ones are—Subdeacons, acolytes, exorcists, readers, and doorkeepers: all of them as early as the third century. Four others, including singers, are somewhat later. Besides these, there were some classes of officers (including those mentioned in Can. II.) who with the exception of the steward might be laymen. See Bingham, bk. iii.

[q] See Bingham, bk. xxiii. ii. 1.

πρόσωπον τῷ ὀρθοδόξῳ. εἰ δέ τις τοῦτον τὸν ὅρον παραβαίη τῆς ἁγίας συνόδου, κανονικῷ ὑποκείσθω ἐπιτιμίῳ.

ΚΑΝΩΝ ΙΕ.

Διάκονον μὴ χειροτονεῖσθαι γυναῖκα πρὸ ἐτῶν τεσσαράκοντα, καὶ ταύτην μετὰ ἀκριβοῦς δοκιμασίας. εἰ δέ γε δεξαμένη τὴν χειροθεσίαν, καὶ χρόνον τινὰ παραμείνασα τῇ λειτουργίᾳ, ἑαυτὴν ἐπιδῷ γάμῳ, ὑβρίσασα τὴν τοῦ Θεοῦ χάριν, ἡ τοιαύτη ἀναθεματιζέσθω μετὰ τοῦ αὐτῇ συναφθέντος.

ΚΑΝΩΝ Ιϛ.

Παρθένον ἑαυτὴν ἀναθεῖσαν τῷ δεσπότῃ Θεῷ, ὡσαύτως δὲ καὶ μονάζοντας, μὴ ἐξεῖναι γάμῳ προσομιλεῖν· εἰ δε γε εὑρεθεῖεν τοῦτο ποιοῦντες, ἔστωσαν ἀκοινώνητοι. ὡρίσαμεν δὲ ἔχειν τὴν αὐθεντίαν τῆς ἐπ' αὐτοῖς φιλανθρωπίας τὸν κατὰ τόπον ἐπίσκοπον.

ΚΑΝΩΝ ΙΖ.

Τὰς καθ' ἑκάστην ἐκκλησίαν ἀγροικικὰς παροικίας ἢ ἐγχωρίους, μένειν ἀπαρασαλεύτους παρὰ τοῖς κατέχουσιν αὐτὰς ἐπισκόποις, καὶ μάλιστα εἰ τριακονταετῆ χρόνον ταύτας ἀβιάστως διακατέχοντες ᾠκονόμησαν. εἰ δὲ ἐντὸς τῶν τριάκοντα ἐτῶν γεγένηταί τις, ἢ γένοιτο περὶ αὐτῶν ἀμφισβήτησις, ἐξεῖναι τοῖς λέγουσιν ἠδικῆσθαι περὶ τούτων, κινεῖν παρὰ τῇ συνόδῳ τῆς ἐπαρχίας. εἰ δέ τις παρὰ τοῦ ἰδίου ἀδικοῖτο μητροπολίτου, παρὰ τῷ ἐπάρχῳ τῆς διοικήσεως, ἢ τῷ Κωνσταν-

son shall promise to come over to the orthodox faith. But if any one transgresses this decision of the holy Synod, let him undergo canonical punishment.

XV.
Concerning Deaconesses.

LET not a woman be ordained Deaconess* before she be forty, and that with strict examination; and if after ordination and continuance in ministration she marry, despising the gift of God, let both her and her husband be anathematized.

XVI.
Of Virgins.

A VIRGIN† that has dedicated herself to God, and likewise monks, may not marry. And if they are found to have done this, let them be excommunicated. But we decree, that the Bishop of that place have power of indulgence in such cases.

XVII.
Of Parishes.

OUTLYING and country parishes in every Church are to remain undisturbed to those Bishops who have held them, especially if they have been peaceably possessed of them for thirty years past: but if there has been or shall be any dispute within thirty years, then those who say they are aggrieved may make application to the provincial Synod. But if any one be wronged by his Metropolitan, let his cause be tried by the Exarch of

---

* Rom. xvi. 1; Canon Laod. ii.; 1 Tim. vi. 10, refers to a higher order.
† There were two kinds of sacred virgins, of which one was not bound by a vow. See Bingham, bk. vii. 4.

τινουπόλεως θρόνῳ δικαζέσθω, καθὰ προείρηται. εἰ δέ τις ἐκ βασιλικῆς ἐξουσίας ἐκαίνισθη πόλις ἢ αὖθις καινισθείη, τοῖς πολιτικοῖς καὶ δημοσίοις τύποις καὶ τῶν ἐκκλησιαστικῶν παροικιῶν ἡ τάξις ἀκολουθείτω.

ΚΑΝΩΝ ΙΗ.

Τὸ τῆς συνωμοσίας ἢ φρατρίας ἔγκλημα, καὶ παρὰ τῶν ἔξω νόμων πάντη κεκώλυται, πολλῷ δὴ μᾶλλον ἐν τῇ τοῦ Θεοῦ ἐκκλησίᾳ τοῦτο γίνεσθαι ἀπαγορεύειν προσήκει. εἴ τινες τοίνυν ἢ κληρικοὶ ἢ μονάζοντες εὑρεθεῖεν, ἢ συνομνύμενοι ἢ φρατριάζοντες, ἢ κατασκευὰς τυρεύοντες ἐπισκόποις ἢ συγκληρικοῖς ἐκπιπτέτωσαν πάντη τοῦ οἰκείου βαθμοῦ.

ΚΑΝΩΝ ΙΘ.

Ἦλθεν εἰς τὰς ἡμετέρας ἀκοὰς, ὡς ἐν ταῖς ἐπαρχίαις αἱ κεκανονισμέναι σύνοδοι τῶν ἐπισκόπων οὐ γίνονται, καὶ ἐκ τούτου πολλὰ παραμελεῖται τῶν διορθώσεως δεομένων ἐκκλησιαστικῶν πραγμάτων. ὥρισεν τοίνυν ἡ ἁγία σύνοδος κατὰ τοὺς τῶν ἁγίων πατέρων κανόνας, δὶς τοῦ ἐνιαυτοῦ ἐπὶ τὸ αὐτὸ συντρέχειν καθ᾽ ἑκάστην ἐπαρχίαν τοὺς ἐπισκόπους, ἔνθα ἂν ὁ τῆς μητροπόλεως ἐπίσκοπος δοκιμάσῃ, καὶ διορθοῦν ἕκαστα τὰ ἀνακύπτοντα· τοὺς δὲ μὴ συνιόντας ἐπισκόπους ἐνδημοῦντας ταῖς ἑαυτῶν πόλεσι, καὶ ταῦτα ἐν ὑγείᾳ διάγοντας, καὶ πάσης ἀπαραιτήτου καὶ ἀναγκαίας ἀσχολίας ὄντας ἐλευθέρους, ἀδελφικῶς ἐπιπλήττεσθαι.

the diocese, or the throne of Constantinople, as is aforesaid ⁿ. If any city be new-built by the Emperor, the ordering of the ecclesiastical parishes shall follow the political and civil pattern ˣ.

XVIII.
Of Unlawful Societies.

The crime of conspiracy or banding together is wholly forbid by the civil laws, much more ought it to be forbid in the Church of God. If, therefore, clergymen or monks be found conspiring or banding together, or laying snares against their Bishop or fellow clergy, they shall be deposed from their proper rank.

XIX.
Concerning Provincial Synods.

It has come to our hearing that the Synods of the Bishops which are prescribed by the Canons in the provinces, do not take place: and that from this cause many of the things which are required for the right settlement of ecclesiastical matters are neglected. The holy Synod has therefore determined, according to the Canons ʸ of the holy Fathers, that the Bishops in every province shall meet together twice in every year, at the place which the Bishop of the Metropolis shall approve, and settle whatever matters may have arisen. And that the Bishops who do not come to the meeting, residing in their own cities, and being in good health, and being free from all unavoidable and necessary business, shall be reproved in a brotherly manner.

ⁿ Can. 9.
ˣ In other words, where there is a civil governor there shall also be a Bishop.
ʸ Can. Apostol. 37, Nic. 5, Antioch. 20. The provincial Synod is here supposed to consist of Bishops.

ΚΑΝΩΝ Κ.

Κληρικοὺς εἰς ἐκκλησίαν τελοῦντας, καθὼς ἤδη ὡρίσαμεν, μὴ ἐξεῖναι εἰς ἄλλης πόλεως τάττεσθαι ἐκκλησίαν· ἀλλὰ στέργειν ἐκείνην ἐν ᾗ ἐξ ἀρχῆς λειτουργεῖν ἠξιώθησαν· ἐκτὸς ἐκείνων, οἵτινες ἀπολέσαντες τὰς ἰδίας πατρίδας ἀπὸ ἀνάγκης εἰς ἄλλην ἐκκλησίαν μετῆλθον. εἰ δέ τις ἐπίσκοπος μετὰ τὸν ὅρον τοῦτον, ἄλλῳ ἐπισκόπῳ προσήκοντα δεξῆται κληρικὸν, ἔδοξεν ἀκοινώνητον εἶναι καὶ τὸν δεχθέντα καὶ τὸν δεξάμενον, ἕως ἂν ὁ μεταστὰς κληρικὸς εἰς τὴν ἰδίαν ἐπανέλθῃ ἐκκλησίαν.

ΚΑΝΩΝ ΚΑ.

Κληρικοὺς ἢ λαϊκοὺς κατηγοροῦντας ἐπισκόπων ἢ κληρικῶν, ἁπλῶς καὶ ἀδοκιμάστως μὴ προσδέχεσθαι εἰς κατηγορίαν, εἰ μὴ πρότερον ἐξετασθῇ αὐτῶν ἡ ὑπόληψις.

ΚΑΝΩΝ ΚΒ.

Μὴ ἐξεῖναι κληρικοὺς μετὰ θάνατον τοῦ ἰδίου ἐπισκόπου διαρπάζειν τὰ διαφέροντα αὐτῷ πράγματα, καθὼς καὶ τοῖς πάλαι κανόσιν ἀπηγόρευται· τοὺς δὲ τοῦτο ποιοῦντας κινδυνεύειν εἰς τοὺς ἰδίους βαθμούς.

XX.
Clergy are not to leave their Place.

The clergy who minister in any Church, as we have already determined [a], are not to be allowed to be appointed to the Church of another city, but are to be contented with that in which they have been first counted worthy to minister, excepting those who having been obliged to leave their own country by some necessity, have passed over to another Church. But if any Bishop, after this decree, shall receive a clergyman belonging to another Bishop, it is decreed, that both the received and the receiver shall be excommunicated, until such time as the clergyman who has gone over shall return to his own Church.

XXI.
Of the Accusers of Bishops or Clergy.

That clergymen or laymen who loosely and without proof bring charges against Bishops or clergy be not admitted to accuse them, till their own reputation has been examined [a].

XXII.
Of the Goods of Deceased Bishops.

Clergymen upon the death of their Bishop must not seize what belongs to him, as has been forbidden by former Canons [b]; but those who do this will be in danger of losing their proper rank.

---

[a] Can. Nic. 16, Eph. 1.   [a] Can. Const. 6.
     [b] Can. Apostol. 40; Can. Antioch. 24.

ΚΑΝΩΝ ΚΓ.

Ἦλθεν εἰς τὰς ἀκοὰς τῆς ἁγίας συνόδου, ὡς κληρικοί τινες καὶ μονάζοντες μηδὲν ἐγκεχειρισμένοι ὑπὸ τοῦ ἰδίου ἐπισκόπου, ἔστι δὲ ὅτε καὶ ἀκοινώνητοι γενόμενοι παρ' αὐτοῦ, καταλαμβάνοντες τὴν βασιλεύουσαν Κωνσταντινούπολιν, ἐπὶ πολὺ ἐν αὐτῇ διατρίβουσι, ταραχὰς ἐμποιοῦντες καὶ θορυβοῦντες τὴν ἐκκλησιαστικὴν κατάστασιν, ἀνατρέπουσί τε οἴκους τινῶν. ὥρισεν τοίνυν ἡ ἁγία σύνοδος, τοὺς τοιούτους ὑπομιμνήσκεσθαι μὲν πρότερον διὰ τοῦ ἐκδίκου τῆς κατὰ Κωνσταντινούπολιν ἁγιωτάτης ἐκκλησίας ἐπὶ τὸ ἐξελθεῖν τῆς βασιλευούσης πόλεως. εἰ δὲ τοῖς αὐτοῖς πράγμασιν ἐπιμένοιεν ἀναισχυντοῦντες, καὶ ἄκοντας αὐτοὺς διὰ τοῦ αὐτοῦ ἐκδίκου ἐκβάλλεσθαι, καὶ τοὺς ἰδίους καταλαμβάνειν τόπους.

ΚΑΝΩΝ ΚΔ.

Τὰ ἅπαξ καθιερωθέντα μοναστήρια κατὰ γνώμην ἐπισκόπου, μένειν εἰς τὸ διηνεκὲς μοναστήρια, καὶ τὰ προσήκοντα αὐτοῖς πράγματα φυλάττεσθαι τῷ μοναστηρίῳ, καὶ μηκέτι δύνασθαι γίνεσθαι ταῦτα κοσμικὰ καταγώγια. τοὺς δὲ συγχωροῦντας τοῦτο γίνεσθαι, ὑποκεῖσθαι τοῖς ἐκ τῶν κανόνων ἐπιτιμίοις.

ΚΑΝΩΝ ΚΕ.

Ἐπειδήπέρ τινες τῶν μητροπολιτῶν, ὡς περιηχήθημεν, ἀμελοῦσι τῶν ἐγκεχειρισμένων αὐτοῖς ποιμνίων, καὶ ἀναβάλ-

XXIII.
Those Excommunicated are to be Subject to Discipline.

It has come to the hearing of the holy Synod, that certain clergymen and monks, without any authority from their own Bishop, and perhaps excommunicated by him, run to the royal city of Constantinople, and, remaining there for a long time, raise seditions, and disturb the Ecclesiastical State, subverting men's houses. The holy Synod has decreed that such persons shall first be warned by the Defensor[c] of the most holy Church of Constantinople, to get them gone out of the Imperial City; and if they shamelessly continue in the same practices, they are to be thrust out against their wills by the said Defensor, and to return to their own place.

XXIV.
Monasteries not to be Secularized.

The monasteries which have been once consecrated[d] with the sanction of the Bishop, are to remain monasteries for ever, and the goods that belong to them are to be preserved in the monastery, and they are no more to become secular dwelling-places. But those who suffer this to be done shall undergo the canonical penalties.

XXV.
Consecration of Bishops not to be Put Off.

Forasmuch as some Metropolitans, as we hear, neglect the flocks committed to them, and put off the consecra-

---
[c] See note on Can. XIV.
[d] *Corp. Jur. Civ. Instit.*, ii. 1. 8, from which it is clear that even "the ground on which a sacred edifice has once been erected, even after the building has been destroyed, continues to be sacred." —Ed. Sandars, p. 170.

λονται τὰς χειροτονίας τῶν ἐπισκόπων· ἔδοξε τῇ ἁγίᾳ συνόδῳ ἐντὸς τριῶν μηνῶν γίνεσθαι τὰς χειροτονίας τῶν ἐπισκύπων, εἰ μή ποτε ἄρα ἀπαραίτητος ἀνάγκη παρασκευάσῃ ἐπιταθῆναι τὸν τῆς ἀναβολῆς χρόνον. εἰ δὲ μὴ τοῦτο ποιήσῃ, ὑποκεῖσθαι αὐτὸν ἐκκλησιαστικῷ ἐπιτιμίῳ, τὴν μέν τοι πρόσοδον τῆς χηρευούσης ἐκκλησίας σώαν παρὰ τῷ οἰκονόμῳ τῆς αὐτῆς ἐκκλησίας φυλάττεσθαι.

ΚΑΝΩΝ Κϛ.

Ἐπειδὴ δὲ ἔν τισιν ἐκκλησίαις, ὡς περιηχήθημεν, δίχα οἰκονόμων οἱ ἐπίσκοποι τὰ ἐκκλησιαστικὰ χειρίζουσι πράγματα· ἔδοξε πᾶσαν ἐκκλησίαν ἐπίσκοπον ἔχουσαν καὶ οἰκονόμον ἔχειν ἐκ τοῦ ἰδίου κλήρου· οἰκονομοῦντα τὰ ἐκκλησιαστικὰ κατὰ γνώμην τοῦ ἰδίου ἐπισκόπου· ὥστε μὴ ἀμάρτυρον εἶναι τὴν οἰκονομίαν τῆς ἐκκλησίας, καὶ ἐκ τούτου τὰ τῆς αὐτῆς ἐκκλησίας σκορπίζεσθαι πράγματα, καὶ λοιδορίαν τῇ ἱερωσύνῃ προστρίβεσθαι· εἰ δὲ μὴ τοῦτο ποιήσοι, ὑποκεῖσθαι αὐτὸν τοῖς θείοις κανόσιν.

ΚΑΝΩΝ ΚΖ.

Τοὺς ἁρπάζοντας γυναῖκας καὶ ἐπ' ὀνόματι συνοικεσίου, ἢ συμπράττοντας ἢ συναιροῦντας τοῖς ἁρπάζουσιν, ὥρισεν ἡ ἁγία σύνοδος, εἰ μὲν κληρικοὶ εἶεν, ἐκπίπτειν τοῦ οἰκείου βαθμοῦ· εἰ δὲ λαϊκοί, ἀναθεματίζεσθαι αὐτούς.

ΨΗΦΟΣ τῆς αὐτῆς ἁγίας συνόδου, ἐκφωνηθεῖσα χάριν τῶν πρεσβείων τοῦ θρόνου τῆς ἁγιωτάτης ἐκκλησίας Κωνσταντινουπόλεως.

tion of Bishops, the holy Synod has decreed that the laying on of hands on Bishops take place within three months, except some invincible necessity require that the time be lengthened, but if he shall not do this he shall suffer ecclesiastical penalty. And that the revenues of the widowed Church be secured by the Œconomus*.

XXVI.
Of Diocesan Stewards.

WHEREAS in some Churches, as we have heard, the Bishops manage the ecclesiastical estate without Stewards, the holy Synod decrees, that every Bishop's Church have an Œconomus out of its own clergy, who shall manage the ecclesiastical estate at the direction of the Bishop, that so the administration of the Church be not without witness, and by this means the goods of the Church be not wasted, and reproach brought upon the priesthood. He that does not comply, let him undergo the sentence of the divine Canons.

XXVII.
Of Ravishers of Women.

THE holy Synod has decreed that they who take women by force under pretence of marriage, and their accomplices or co-ravishers, are to be deposed, if clergymen; anathematized, if laymen.

THE DECREE OF THE SAME HOLY SYNOD PROMULGATED ON ACCOUNT OF THE PRIVILEGES OF THE THRONE OF THE MOST HOLY CHURCH OF CONSTANTINOPLE.

---

* See note on Can. XIV. and Can. Antioch. 25. This is probably the beginning of the office of Archdeacon.

ΚΑΝΩΝ ΚΗ.

Πανταχοῦ τοῖς τῶν ἁγίων πατέρων ὅροις ἑπόμενοι, καὶ τὸν ἀρτίως ἀναγνωσθέντα κανόνα τῶν ἑκατὸν πεντήκοντα θεοφιλεστάτων ἐπισκόπων, τῶν συναχθέντων ἐπὶ τοῦ τῆς εὐσεβοῦς μνήμης μεγάλου Θεοδοσίου τοῦ γενομένου βασιλέως ἐν τῇ βασιλίδι Κωνσταντινουπόλει νέᾳ Ῥώμῃ, γνωρίζοντες, τὰ αὐτὰ καὶ ἡμεῖς ὁρίζομέν τε καὶ ψηφιζόμεθα περὶ τῶν πρεσβείων τῆς ἁγιωτάτης ἐκκλησίας τῆς αὐτῆς Κωνσταντινουπόλεως νέας Ῥώμης. καὶ γὰρ τῷ θρόνῳ τῆς πρεσβυτέρας Ῥώμης, διὰ τὸ βασιλεύειν τὴν πόλιν ἐκείνην οἱ πατέρες εἰκότως ἀποδεδώκασι τὰ πρεσβεῖα· καὶ τῷ αὐτῷ σκοπῷ κινούμενοι οἱ ἑκατὸν πεντήκοντα θεοφιλέστατοι ἐπίσκοποι, τὰ ἴσα πρεσβεῖα ἀπένειμαν τῷ τῆς νέας Ῥώμης ἁγιωτάτῳ θρόνῳ, εὐλόγως κρίναντες, τὴν βασιλείᾳ καὶ συγκλήτῳ τιμηθεῖσαν πόλιν, καὶ τῶν ἴσων ἀπολαύουσαν πρεσβείων τῇ πρεσβυτέρᾳ βασιλίδι Ῥώμῃ, καὶ ἐν τοῖς ἐκκλησιαστικοῖς ὡς ἐκείνην μεγαλύνεσθαι πράγμασι, δευτέραν μετ' ἐκείνην ὑπάρχουσαν. καὶ ὥστε τοὺς τῆς Ποντικῆς καὶ τῆς Ἀσιανῆς καὶ τῆς Θρακικῆς διοικήσεως μητροπολίτας μόνους, ἔτι δὲ καὶ τοὺς ἐν τοῖς βαρβαρικοῖς ἐπισκόπους τῶν προειρημένων διοικήσεων χειροτονεῖσθαι ὑπὸ τοῦ προειρημένου ἁγιωτάτου θρόνου τῆς κατὰ Κωνσταντινούπολιν ἁγιωτάτης ἐκκλησίας· δηλαδὴ ἑκάστου μητροπολίτου τῶν προειρημένων διοικήσεων μετὰ τῶν τῆς ἐπαρχίας ἐπισκόπων χειροτονοῦντος τοὺς τῆς ἐπαρχίας ἐπισκόπους, καθὼς τοῖς θείοις κανόσι διηγόρευται. χειροτονεῖσθαι δὲ, καθὼς εἴρηται τοὺς μητροπολίτας τῶν προειρημένων διοικήσεων παρὰ τοῦ Κωνσταντινουπόλεως ἀρχιεπισκόπου, ψηφισμάτων συμφώνων κατὰ τὸ ἔθος γενομένων, καὶ ἐπ' αὐτὸν ἀναφερομένων.

XXVIII.[1]

WE, following in all things the decisions of the holy Fathers, and acknowledging the Canon of the 150 most religious Bishops which has just been read, do also determine and decree the same things respecting the privileges of the most holy city of Constantinople, which is new Rome. For the Fathers properly gave the Primacy to the throne of the elder Rome, because that was the imperial city. And the 150 most religious Bishops, being moved with the same intention, gave equal privileges to the most holy throne of new Rome, judging with reason, that the city which was honoured with the sovereignty and senate, and which enjoyed equal privileges with the elder royal Rome, should also be magnified like her in ecclesiastical matters, being the second after her. And that the Metropolitans only of the Pontic, and Asian, and Thracian dioceses, and moreover the Bishops of the aforesaid dioceses who are amongst the barbarians, shall be ordained by the above-mentioned most holy throne of the most holy Church of Constantinople; each Metropolitan of the aforesaid dioceses ordaining the Bishops of the province, as has been declared by the divine Canons; but the Metropolitans themselves of the said dioceses shall, as has been said, be ordained by the Bishop of Constantinople, the proper elections being made according to custom, and reported to him.

[1] By this Act of the Council the Bishop of Constantinople first obtained the rank of Patriarch. It was not drawn up as a Canon by the Fathers of this Council, nor does it exist in all the collections. The fact, however, of the opposition made to it by the Roman Legates proves its authenticity. An abridged account of the proceedings is to be found in Hammond, pp. 109, 111. The Council, which in its definition of faith was guided by St. Leo, here, in a matter of order, follows what would seem to be Imperial influence. See Routh, Opuscula, pp. 470, 1; Socrates, Hist. Eccl., ii. 17; Sozomen, iii. 10.

ΤΗΣ αὐτῆς ἁγίας συνόδου ἐκ τῆς πράξεως τῆς περὶ Φωτίου ἐπισκόπου Τύρου καὶ Εὐσταθίου ἐπισκόπου Βηρίτου.

Οἱ μεγαλοπρεπέστατοι καὶ ἐνδυξότατοι ἄρχοντες εἶπον.

Περὶ τῶν ἐπισκόπων τῶν χειροτονηθέντων μὲν παρὰ Φωτίου τοῦ εὐλαβεστάτου ἐπισκόπου, ἀποκινηθέντων δὲ παρὰ Εὐσταθίου τοῦ εὐλαβεστάτου ἐπισκόπου, καὶ μετὰ τὴν ἐπισκοπὴν πρεσβυτέρων εἶναι κελευσθέντων, τί παρίσταται τῇ ἁγίᾳ συνόδῳ;

Πασκασῖνος καὶ Λουκήνσιος, οἱ εὐλαβέστατοι ἐπίσκοποι, καὶ Βωνηφάτιος πρεσβύτερος, τοποτηρηταὶ τῆς ἐκκλησίας Ῥώμης εἶπον.

ΚΑΝΩΝ ΚΘ.

Ἐπίσκοπον εἰς πρεσβυτέρου βαθμὸν φέρειν, ἱεροσυλία ἐστίν. εἰ δὲ αἰτία τὶς δικαία ἐκείνους ἀπὸ τῆς πράξεως τῆς ἐπισκοπῆς ἀποκινεῖ· οὐδὲ πρεσβυτέρου τόπον κατέχειν ὀφείλουσιν. εἰ δὲ ἐκτός τινος ἐγκλήματος ἀπεκινήθησαν τοῦ ἀξιώματος, πρὸς τὴν ἐπισκοπικὴν ἀξίαν ἐπαναστρέψουσιν.

ΑΝΑΤΟΛΙΟΣ ὁ εὐλαβέστατος ἀρχιεπίσκοπος Κωνσταντινουπόλεως εἶπεν.

Οὗτοι οἱ λεγόμενοι ἀπὸ τῆς ἐπισκοπῆς ἀξίας εἰς τὴν τοῦ πρεσβυτέρου τάξιν κατεληλυθέναι, εἰ μὲν ἀπὸ εὐλόγων αἰτιῶν καταδικάζονται· εἰκότως οὐδὲ τῆς πρεσβυτέρου ἐντὸς ἄξιοι τυγχάνουσιν εἶναι τιμῆς. εἰ δὲ δίχα τινὸς αἰτίας εὐλόγου εἰς τὸν ἥττονα κατεβιβάσθησαν βαθμὸν, δίκαιοι τυγχάνουσιν, εἴγε ἀνεύθυνοι φανεῖεν· τὴν τῆς ἐπισκοπῆς ἐπαναλαβεῖν ἀξίαν τε καὶ ἱερωσύνην.

THE CHALCEDON CANONS.   75

From the Acts of the same holy Synod in the matter of Photius, Bishop of Tyre, and Eustathius Bishop of Berytus.

The great men and illustrious rulers said:—

What is determined by the holy Synod concerning the bishops ordained by the most religious Bishop Photius, and seconded by the most religious Eustathius, and ordered to be under the oversight of Priests?

The most religious Bishops Pascasinus and Lucensius, with the Priest Boniface representing the Church of Rome said:—

XXIX.[g]

It is sacrilege to degrade Bishops into the order of Priests. If for any just cause they are removed from the episcopal function, they deserve not the character of Priests; if without cause they are depressed to a lower degree, they shall be restored to their dignity.

Anatolius, the most religious Archbishop of Constantinople said, Those who are declared to have descended from the episcopal dignity to the order of Priest, if indeed they are condemned for just causes, are not rightly worthy of the honour[h] of a Priest. But if without any reasonable cause they have been thrust down to the lower rank, let them recover of right, if they appear guiltless, both the authority of the episcopate, and also the priesthood[i].

---

[g] This Canon also, as well as the following one, is more properly a Synodical decree, passed to settle a local disturbance; a full account of the matter is given at the end of the fourth Act of the Council.

[h] Or *pay*, cf. 1 Tim. v. 17.

[i] St. Luke i. 8, 9; Heb. v. 10, vii. 1.

Πάντες οἱ εὐλαβέστατοι ἐπίσκοποι ἐβόησαν.

Δικαία ἡ κρίσις τῶν πατέρων. πάντες τὰ αὐτὰ λέγομεν· οἱ πατέρες δικαίως ἐψηφίσαντο· ἡ ψῆφος τῶν ἀρχιεπισκόπων κρατείτω.

Οἱ μεγαλοπρέστατοι καὶ ἐνδοξότατοι ἄρχοντες εἶπον·

Τὰ ἀρέσαντα τῇ ἁγίᾳ συνόδῳ εἰς τὸν ἅπαντα χρόνον βέβαια φυλαττέσθω.

ΤΗΣ αὐτῆς ἁγίας συνόδου ἐκ τῆς τετάρτης πράξεως, ἔνθα σκοπεῖται τὸ κεφάλαιον τὸ κατὰ τοὺς ἐπισκόπους Αἰγύπτου·

Οἱ μεγαλοπρεπέστατοι καὶ ἐνδοξύτατοι ἄρχοντες, καὶ ἡ ὑπερφυὴς σύγκλητος εἶπον.

ΚΑΝΩΝ Λ.

Ἐπειδὴ οἱ εὐλαβέστατοι ἐπίσκοποι τῆς Αἰγύπτου, οὐχ' ὡς μαχόμενοι τῇ καθολικῇ πίστει, ὑπογράψαι τῇ ἐπιστολῇ τοῦ ὁσιωτάτου ἀρχιεπισκόπου Λέοντος ἐπὶ τοῦ παρόντος ἀνεβάλλοντο, ἀλλὰ φάσκοντες ἔθος εἶναι ἐν τῇ Αἰγυπτιακῇ διοικήσει παρὰ γνώμην καὶ διατύπωσιν τοῦ ἀρχιεπισκόπου μηδὲν τοιοῦτο ποιεῖν· καὶ ἀξιοῦσιν ἐνδοθῆναι αὐτοῖς ἄχρι τῆς χειροτονίας τοῦ ἐσομένου τῆς Ἀλεξανδρέων μεγαλοπόλεως ἐπισκόπου. Εὔλογον ἡμῖν ἐφάνη καὶ φιλάνθρωπον, ὥστε αὐτοῖς μένουσιν ἐπὶ τοῦ οἰκείου σχήματος ἐν τῇ βασιλευούσῃ πόλει, ἔνδοσιν παρασχεθῆναι, ἄχρις ἂν χειροτονηθῇ ὁ ἀρχιεπίσκοπος τῆς Ἀλεξανδρέων μεγαλοπόλεως.

All the most religious prelates declared aloud, "Just is the judgment of the Fathers: We all say the same. The Fathers have rightly decreed; Let the decree of the Archbishops hold good."

The great men and illustrious rulers said, "Let the pleasure of the holy Synod be established and remain fixed for ever."

From the fourth Act of the same holy Synod, when was to be considered the matter of the Egyptian Bishops.

The great men and illustrious rulers, and the great legislative assembly, said,—

XXX.

Since the most religious Bishops of Egypt have put off for the present subscribing the Epistle [k] of the most holy Archbishop Leo, not as contending against the Catholic faith, but saying that it is the custom of the Egyptian diocese to do nothing of the sort without the sanction and order of the Archbishop, and therefore requesting that they may be allowed to defer their subscription till the ordination of the future Archbishop of the great city of Alexandria, it has appeared to us reasonable and humane that this concession should be made to them, upon their remaining in their proper habit in the imperial city, until the Archbishop of the great city of Alexandria shall be ordained.

[k] Commonly called the Tome of St. Leo; an exposition of the Catholic faith addressed by the Pope to the Council, and in conformity with which the definition of faith was drawn up. It is printed in Mr. Bright's edition of St. Leo's "Sermons on the Incarnation," and portions of it appear in an English version at the end of the "History of the Church," by the same author.

ΠΑΣΚΑΣΙΝΟΣ ὁ εὐλαβέστατος ἐπίσκοπος τοποτηρητὴς τοῦ ἀποστολικοῦ θρόνου Ῥώμης, εἶπεν.

Εἰ προστάττει ἡ ὑμετέρα ἐξουσία, καὶ κελεύεταί τί ποτε αὐτοῖς παρασχεθῆναι φιλανθρωπίας ἐχόμενον, ἐγγύας δότωσαν, ὅτι οὐκ ἐξέρχωνται ταύτης τῆς πόλεως, ἕως οὗ ἡ Ἀλεξανδρέων πόλις ἐπίσκοπον δέξηται.

Οἱ μεγαλοπρεπέστατοι καὶ ἐνδοξότατοι ἄρχοντες, καὶ ἡ ὑπερφυὴς σύγκλητος εἶπον.

Ἡ τοῦ ὁσιωτάτου Πασκασίνου ψῆφος βεβαία ἔστω, ὅθεν μένοντες ἐπὶ τοῦ οἰκείου σχήματος οἱ εὐλαβέστατοι ἐπίσκοποι τῶν Αἰγυπτίων, ἢ ἐγγύας παρέξουσιν, εἰ τοῦτο αὐτοῖς δυνατόν, ἢ ἐξωμοσίᾳ καταπιστευθήσονται ἀναμένειν τὴν χειροτονίαν τοῦ ἐσομένου ἐπισκόπου τῆς Ἀλεξανδρέων μεγαλοπόλεως.

ΤΗΣ αὐτῆς ἁγίας συνόδου ἐκ τῆς τετάρτης πράξεως.

Ἡ ἁγία καὶ οἰκουμενικὴ καὶ μακαρία σύνοδος τῶν τριακοσίων δεκαοκτὼ τῆς πίστεως τὸν κανόνα τὸν ἐν τῇ Νικαίᾳ παρὰ αὐτῶν ἐκτεθέντα, καὶ τοῖς ὅροις κρατεῖ καὶ μεταδιώκει. οὐ μὴν ἀλλὰ καὶ ἡ τῶν ἑκατὸν πεντήκοντα συναχθεῖσα σύνοδος ἐν τῇ Κωνσταντινουπόλει ἐπὶ τοῦ τῆς μακαρίας μνήμης Θεοδοσίου τοῦ μεγάλου, τὴν αὐτὴν πίστιν ἐβεβαίωσεν. οὗ τινος συμβόλου τὴν ἔκθεσιν ἡ ἐπὶ τοῦ ἐν μακαρίᾳ τῇ μνήμῃ Κυρίλλου σύνοδος ἐν τῇ Ἐφέσῳ ἐξενεχθεῖσα ἐν ᾗ Νεστόριος κατεδικάσθη, ὁμοίως ἀσπάζεται. Τρίτον δὲ τοῦ μακαριωτάτου ἀνδρός, πασῶν τῶν ἐκκλησιῶν ἀρχιεπισκόπου Λέοντος, τοῦ Νεστορίου, καὶ Εὐτυχοῦς αἵρεσιν καταδικάσαντος τὰ ἀποσταλέντα γράμματα φανεροῦσι ποία τῆς ἀληθείας ἡ πίστις. ὁμοίως δὲ καὶ ἡ ἁγία σύνοδος ταύτην τὴν πίστιν κατέχει, ταύτην μεταδιώκει.

The most religious Bishop Pascasinus, legate of the Apostolic see of Rome, said, "If your authority ordain and command that concession which was formerly made to them, let them give sureties that they will not go out of this city until the city of Alexandria receives a Bishop."

The great men, and illustrious rulers, and the great Synod, answered, "Let the decree of the most devout Pascasinus be confirmed; so that the most religious Egyptian Bishops remaining in their proper dignity will either offer securities, if that be possible, or will bind themselves by an oath to await the consecration of the new bishop of Alexandria.

CONFIRMATION OF FORMER CREEDS AND AUTHORIZED EXPOSITIONS OF THE FAITH: FROM THE FOURTH ACT OF THE COUNCIL.

THIS holy, œcumenical, and blessed Synod follows and holds the rule of faith laid down by the 318 fathers at Nicæa, which also the Synod of the 150 gathered at Constantinople under Theodosius of blessed memory confirmed. And it further embraces the exposition of the faith set forth at Ephesus by Cyril of blessed memory, when Nestorius was condemned: and thirdly the letter addressed by the blessed and apostolic Leo, Archbishop of all the Churches, condemning the heresy of Nestorius and Eutyches. In like manner this holy Synod holds this faith, this faith it follows.

DEFINITIO FIDEI
APUD CONCILIUM CHALCEDONIUM.

Η ἉΓΙΑ καὶ μεγάλη καὶ οἰκουμενικὴ σύνοδος, ἡ κατὰ Θεοῦ χάριν καὶ θέσπισμα τῶν εὐσεβεστάτων καὶ φιλοχρίστων ἡμῶν βασιλέων Μαρκιανοῦ καὶ Οὐαλεντιανοῦ Αὐγούστων, συναχθεῖσα ἐν τῇ Καλχηδονέων, μητροπόλει τῆς Βιθυνῶν ἐπαρχίας, ἐν τῷ μαρτυρίῳ τῆς ἁγίας καὶ καλλινίκου μάρτυρος Εὐφημίας, ὥρισε τὰ ὑποτεταγμένα.

Ὁ ΚΥΡΙΟΣ ἡμῶν καὶ σωτὴρ Ἰησοῦς Χριστὸς τῆς πίστεως τὴν γνῶσιν τοῖς μαθηταῖς βεβαιῶν, ἔφη· Εἰρήνην τὴν ἐμὴν ἀφίημι ὑμῖν, εἰρήνην τὴν ἐμὴν δίδωμι ὑμῖν· ὥστε μηδένα πρὸς τὸν πλησίον διαφωνεῖν ἐν τοῖς δόγμασι τῆς εὐσεβείας, ἀλλ᾿ ἐπίσης ἅπασι τὸ τῆς ἀληθείας ἐπιδείκνυσθαι κήρυγμα. ἐπειδὴ δὲ οὐ παύεται διὰ τῶν ἑαυτοῦ ζιζανίων ὁ πονηρὸς τοῖς τῆς εὐσεβείας ἐπιφυόμενος σπέρμασι, καὶ τι καινὸν κατὰ τῆς ἀληθείας ἐφευρίσκων ἀεί, διὰ τοῦτο συνήθως ὁ Δεσπότης προνοούμενος τοῦ ἀνθρωπίνου γένους, τὸν εὐσεβῆ τοῦτον καὶ πιστότατον πρὸς ζῆλον ἀνέστησε βασιλέα, καὶ τοὺς ἀπανταχῇ τῆς ἱερωσύνης πρὸς ἑαυτὸν ἀρχηγοὺς συνεκάλεσεν· ὥστε, τῆς χάριτος τοῦ πάντων ἡμῶν δεσπότου Χριστοῦ ἐνεργούσης, πᾶσαν μὲν τοῦ ψεύδους τῶν τοῦ Χριστοῦ προβάτων ἀποσείσασθαι λύμην, τοῖς δὲ τῆς ἀληθείας αὐτὴν καταπιαίνειν βλαστήμασιν. ὃ δὴ καὶ πεποιήκαμεν, κοινῇ ψήφῳ τὰ τῆς πλάνης

THE DEFINITION OF FAITH,
AGREED UPON AT THE COUNCIL OF CHALCEDON.

THE holy, great, and Œcumenical Synod, assembled by the grace of God, and according to the ordinance of our most religious and Christian Sovereigns, Marcian and Valentinus, in Chalcedon, the Metropolis of the Bithynians, in the Church of the holy and victorious martyr Euphemia, has defined as follows.

Our Lord and Saviour Jesus Christ, in confirming the knowledge of the faith to His disciples, said, "My peace I leave with you, My peace I give unto you;" to the end that no one should speak differently from another in the doctrines of religion, but should set forth equally, to all, the preaching of the truth. Since, however, the evil one does not cease from endeavouring to sow his tares amongst the seeds of godliness, and is continually inventing something new against the truth, therefore the Lord, as He is wont, in His good providence for the human race, has raised up our religious and most zealously faithful Sovereign, and has called together unto him the chief of the priesthood from every quarter, that by the power of the grace of Christ, the Lord of us all, they may remove every plague of falsehood from the sheep of Christ, and nourish them with the fresh leaves of truth. This accordingly we have done, having by our common decree driven away the erroneous doctrines, and having

ἀπελάσαντες δόγματα, τὴν δὲ ἀπλανῆ τῶν πατέρων ἀνανεωσάμενοι πίστιν, τὸ τῶν τριακοσίων δεκαοκτὼ σύμβολον τοῖς πᾶσι κηρύξαντες, καὶ ὡς οἰκείους τοὺς τοῦτο τὸ σύνθεμα τῆς εὐσεβείας δεξαμένους πατέρας ἐπιγραψάμενοι. οἵπερ εἰσὶν οἱ μετὰ ταῦτα ἐν τῇ μεγάλῃ Κωνσταντινουπόλει συνελθόντες ρν΄. καὶ αὐτοὶ τὴν αὐτὴν ἐπισφραγισάμενοι πίστιν. ὁρίζομεν τοίνυν, τὴν τάξιν καὶ τοὺς περὶ τῆς πίστεως ἅπαντας τύπους φυλάττοντες καὶ ἡμεῖς τῆς κατ' Ἔφεσον πάλαι γεγενημένης ἁγίας συνόδου, ἧς ἡγεμόνες οἱ ἁγιώτατοι τὴν μνήμην Κελεστῖνος ὁ τῆς Ῥωμαίων, καὶ Κύριλλος ὁ τῆς Ἀλεξανδρέων, ἐτύγχανον, προλάμπειν μὲν τῆς ὀρθῆς καὶ ἀμωμήτου πίστεως τὴν ἔκθεσιν τῶν τιη΄. ἁγίων καὶ μακαρίων πατέρων τῶν ἐν Νικαίᾳ ἐπὶ τοῦ εὐσεβοῦς μνήμης Κωνσταντίνου τοῦ γενομένου βασιλέως συναχθέντων· κρατεῖν δὲ καὶ τὰ παρὰ τῶν ρν΄. ἁγίων πατέρων ἐν Κωνσταντινουπόλει ὁρισθέντα, πρὸς ἀναίρεσιν μὲν τῶν τότε φυεισῶν αἱρέσεων, βεβαίωσιν δὲ τῆς αὐτῆς καθολικῆς καὶ ἀποστολικῆς ἡμῶν πίστεως.

ΠΙΣΤΕΥΟΜΕΝ κ. τ. λ.

Ἤρκει μὲν οὖν εἰς ἐντελῆ τῆς εὐσεβείας ἐπίγνωσίν τε καὶ βεβαίωσιν τὸ σοφὸν καὶ σωτήριον τοῦτο τῆς θείας χάριτος σύμβολον· περί τε γὰρ τοῦ Πατρὸς καὶ τοῦ Υἱοῦ καὶ τοῦ ἁγίου Πνεύματος ἐκδιδάσκει τὸ τέλειον, καὶ τοῦ Κυρίου τὴν ἐνανθρώπησιν τοῖς πιστῶς δεχομένοις παρίστησιν. ἀλλ' ἐπειδήπερ οἱ

renewed the unerring faith of our Fathers, by publishing to all the Creed of the three hundred and eighteen; and adding to them as of the same family, the Fathers who have received the same covenant of religion, those hundred and fifty, who afterwards assembled in the great city of Constantinople, and ratified the same faith. We therefore preserving the order, and all the forms concerning the faith of the holy Synod, which was held in Ephesus, of which Celestine of Rome, and Cyril of Alexandria of holy memory, were the leaders, declare that the exposition of the right and blameless faith by the three hundred and eighteen holy and blessed Fathers who were assembled at Nice, in the times of the then Sovereign Constantine of pious memory, should have the first place, and that those things also should be maintained which were defined by the hundred and fifty holy Fathers of Constantinople, for the taking away of the heresies which had then sprung up, and the confirmation of the same our Catholic and Apostolic Faith.

The Creed of the three hundred and eighteen Fathers of Nice.

We believe, &c.

Also the Creed of the hundred and fifty holy Fathers who were assembled at Constantinople.

We believe, &c.

This wise and saving Creed of the Divine grace would be sufficient for the full acknowledgment and confirmation of the true religion; for it teaches completely the perfect doctrine concerning the Father, the Son, and the Holy Spirit, and fully explains the Incarnation of the Lord to those who receive it faithfully.

τῆς ἀληθείας ἀθετεῖν ἐπιχειροῦντες τὸ κήρυγμα, διὰ τῶν οἰκείων αἱρέσεων τὰς κενοφωνίας ἀπέτεκον, οἱ μὲν τὸ τῆς δι' ἡμᾶς τοῦ Κυρίου οἰκονομίας μυστήριον παραφθείρειν τολμῶντες, καὶ τὴν Θεοτόκον ἐπὶ τῆς παρθένου φωνὴν ἀπαρνούμενοι· οἱ δὲ σύγχυσιν καὶ κρᾶσιν εἰσάγοντες, καὶ μίαν εἶναι φύσιν τῆς σαρκὸς καὶ τῆς Θεότητος ἀνοήτως ἀναπλάττοντες, καὶ παθητὴν τοῦ μονογενοῦς τὴν θείαν φύσιν τῇ συγχύσει τερατευόμενοι· διὰ τοῦτο πᾶσαν αὐτοῖς ἀποκλεῖσαι κατὰ τῆς ἀληθείας μηχανὴν βουλομένη ἡ παροῦσα νῦν αὕτη ἁγία μεγάλη καὶ οἰκουμενικὴ σύνοδος, τὸ τοῦ κηρύγματος ἄνωθεν ἀσάλευτον ἐκδιδάσκουσα, ὥρισε προηγουμένως, τῶν τριακοσίων δεκαοκτὼ ἁγίων πατέρων τὴν πίστιν μένειν ἀπαρεγχείρητον. καὶ διὰ μὲν τοὺς τῷ Πνεύματι τῷ ἁγίῳ μαχομένους, τὴν χρόνοις ὕστερον παρὰ τῶν ἐπὶ τῆς βασιλευούσης πόλεως συνελθόντων ἑκατὸν πεντήκοντα ἁγίων πατέρων περὶτῆς τοῦ Πνεύματος οὐσίας παραδοθεῖσαν διδασκαλίαν κυροῖ· ἣν ἐκεῖνοι τοῖς πᾶσιν ἐγνώρισαν, οὐκ ὥς τι λεῖπον τοῖς προλαβοῦσιν ἐπάγοντες, ἀλλὰ τὴν περὶ τοῦ ἁγίου Πνεύματος αὐτῶν ἔννοιαν κατὰ τῶν τὴν αὐτοῦ δεσποτείαν ἀθετεῖν πειρωμένων γραφικαῖς μαρτυρίαις τρανώσαντες. διὰ δὲ τοὺς τὸ τῆς οἰκονομίας παραφθείρειν ἐπιχειροῦντας μυστήριον, καὶ ψιλὸν ἄνθρωπον εἶναι τὸν ἐκ τῆς ἁγίας τεχθέντα Μαρίας ἀναιδῶς

But forasmuch as they who endeavoured to make void the preaching of the truth, have by their particular heresies given rise to vain babblings, some daring to corrupt the mystery of the Lord's Incarnation for us, and refusing to the Virgin the appellation of Theotocos[a], others[b] bringing in a confusion and mixture, and absurdly imagining the nature of the flesh and of the Godhead to be one, and teaching the monstrous doctrine that the divine nature of the Only-begotten was by commixture capable of suffering, therefore the present holy, great, and Œcumenical Synod, wishing to shut out all devices against the truth, and to teach the doctrine which has been unalterably held from the beginning, has in the first place decreed, that the faith of the three hundred and eighteen holy Fathers should remain free from assault. Further, on account of those who in later times have contended against the Holy Spirit, it confirms the doctrine concerning the substance of the Spirit, which was delivered by the hundred and fifty holy Fathers who were assembled in the royal city, which they published, not as adding any thing that was wanting to the things which they had before received, but declaring by written testimonies their sentiments concerning the Holy Spirit, against those who endeavoured to destroy His dominion. And further on account of those who endeavour to corrupt the mystery of the Incarnation, and who impudently utter their vain conceits, that He who was born of the holy Virgin Mary, was a mere man, it has

---

[a] Mother of God; which term was to the Nestorians, what the definition, "Of one substance with the Father," was to the Arians.
[b] The Eutychians. See Hooker, Eccl. Pol., liv. 10.

ληρωδοῦντας, τὰς τοῦ μακαρίου Κυρίλλου, τοῦ τῆς Ἀλεξανδρέων ἐκκλησίας γενομένου ποιμένος, συνοδικὰς ἐπιστολὰς πρὸς Νεστόριον καὶ πρὸς τοὺς τῆς ἀνατολῆς, ἁρμοδίους οὔσας ἐδέξατο, εἰς ἔλεγχον μὲν τῆς Νεστορίου φρενοβλαβείας, ἑρμηνείαν δὲ τῶν ἐν εὐσεβεῖ ζήλῳ τοῦ σωτηρίου συμβόλου ποθούντων τὴν ἔννοιαν· αἷς καὶ τὴν ἐπιστολὴν τοῦ τῆς μεγίστης καὶ πρεσβυτέρας Ῥώμης προέδρου τοῦ μακαριωτάτου καὶ ἁγιωτάτου ἀρχιεπισκόπου Λέοντος, τὴν γραφεῖσαν πρὸς τὸν ἐν ἁγίοις ἀρχιεπίσκοπον Φλαυιανὸν ἐπ᾽ ἀναιρέσει τῆς Εὐτυχοῦς κακονοίας, ἅτε δὴ τῇ τοῦ μεγάλου Πέτρου ὁμολογίᾳ συμβαίνουσαν, καὶ κοινήν τινα στήλην ὑπάρχουσαν κατὰ τῶν κακοδοξούντων, εἰκότως συνήρμοσε πρὸς τὴν τῶν ὀρθοδόξων δογμάτων βεβαίωσιν. τοῖς τε γὰρ εἰς υἱῶν δυάδα τὸ τῆς οἰκονομίας διασπᾶν ἐπιχειροῦσι μυστήριον, παρατάττεται· καὶ τοὺς παθητὴν τοῦ μονογενοῦς λέγειν τολμῶντας τὴν Θεότητα, τοῦ τῶν ἱερῶν ἀπωθεῖται συλλόγου· καὶ τοῖς ἐπὶ τῶν δύο φύσεων τοῦ Χριστοῦ κρᾶσιν, ἢ σύγχυσιν ἐπινοοῦσιν ἀνθίσταται· καὶ τοὺς οὐρανίου, ἢ ἑτέρας τινὸς ὑπάρχειν οὐσίας τὴν ἐξ ἡμῶν ληφθεῖσαν αὐτῷ τοῦ δούλου μορφὴν παραπαίοντας ἐξελαύνει· καὶ τοὺς δύο μὲν πρὸ τῆς ἑνώσεως φύσεις τοῦ Κυρίου μυθεύοντας, μίαν δὲ μετὰ τὴν ἕνωσιν ἀναπλάττοντας ἀναθεματίζει· ἑπόμενοι τοίνυν τοῖς ἁγίοις πατράσιν, ἕνα καὶ τὸν αὐτὸν ὁμολογοῦμεν Υἱὸν τὸν Κύριον ἡμῶν Ἰησοῦν Χριστόν, καὶ συμφώνως ἅπαντες ἐκδιδάσκομεν, τέλειον τὸν αὐτὸν ἐν Θεότητι, τέλειον τὸν αὐτὸν ἐν ἀνθρωπότητι, Θεὸν ἀληθῶς, καὶ ἄνθρωπον ἀληθῶς, τὸν αὐτὸν ἐκ ψυχῆς λογικῆς καὶ σώματος, ὁμοούσιον τῷ Πατρὶ κατὰ τὴν Θεότητα, καὶ ὁμοούσιον τὸν αὐτὸν ἡμῖν

received the Synodal letters of Cyril of blessed memory, Pastor of the Church of Alexandria, to Nestorius, and those of the East, being suitable for the refutation of the frenzied imaginations of Nestorius, and for the instruction of those who with godly zeal desire to understand the saving faith. And in addition to these it has properly added for the confirmation of the orthodox doctrines, the letter of the President of great Rome, the most holy and blessed Archbishop Leo, which was written to the holy Archbishop Flavian, for the removal of the evil opinions of Eutyches, as being agreeable to the confession of the great Peter[e], and being, as it were, a common pillar against those who are of wrong opinions; for it is directed against those who attempt to rend the mystery of the Incarnation into a duad of Sons: and it repels from the sacred congregation those who dare to say that the divinity of the Only-begotten is capable of suffering; and it is opposed to those who imagine a mixture or confusion of the two natures of Christ; and it drives away those who fancy that the form of a servant, which was taken by Him of us, is of an heavenly or any other substance; and it condemns those who speak of two natures of the Lord before the union, and feign one after the union.

We, then, following the holy Fathers, all with one consent, teach men to confess, one and the same Son, our Lord Jesus Christ; the same perfect in Godhead and also perfect in Manhood; truly God, and truly man, of a reasonable soul and body; consubstantial with the Father according to the Godhead, and con-

[e] St. Matt. xvi. 16. The voice of the Council declared, "Peter speaks by Leo. Cyril and Leo teach alike."

κατὰ τὴν ἀνθρωπότητα, κατὰ πάντα ὅμοιον ἡμῖν, χωρὶς ἁμαρτίας· πρὸ αἰώνων μὲν ἐκ τοῦ Πατρὸς γεννηθέντα κατὰ τὴν Θεότητα, ἐπ' ἐσχάτων δὲ τῶν ἡμερῶν τὸν αὐτὸν δι' ἡμᾶς καὶ διὰ τὴν ἡμετέραν σωτηρίαν ἐκ Μαρίας τῆς παρθένου τῆς Θεοτόκου κατὰ τὴν ἀνθρωπότητα, ἕνα καὶ τὸν αὐτὸν Χριστὸν, Υἱὸν, Κύριον, μονογενῆ, ἐν δύο φύσεσιν ἀσυγχύτως, ἀτρέπτως, ἀδιαιρέτως, ἀχωρίστως[d] γνωριζόμενον· οὐδαμοῦ τῆς τῶν φύσεων διαφορᾶς ἀνῃρημένης διὰ τὴν ἕνωσιν, σωζομένης δὲ μᾶλλον τῆς ἰδιότητος ἑκατέρας φύσεως, καὶ εἰς ἓν πρόσωπον καὶ μίαν ὑπόστασιν συντρεχούσης, οὐκ εἰς δύο πρόσωπα μεριζόμενον ἢ διαιρούμενον, ἀλλ' ἕνα καὶ τὸν αὐτὸν Υἱὸν καὶ μονογενῆ, Θεὸν λόγον, Κύριον Ἰησοῦν Χριστόν· καθάπερ ἄνωθεν οἱ προφῆται περὶ αὐτοῦ, καὶ αὐτὸς ἡμᾶς ὁ Κύριος Ἰησοῦς Χρστὸς ἐξεπαίδευσε, καὶ τὸ τῶν πατέρων ἡμῖν παραδέδωκε σύμβολον. τούτων τοίνυν μετὰ πάσης πανταχόθεν ἀκριβείας τε καὶ ἐμμελείας παρ' ἡμῶν διατυπωθέντων, ὥρισεν ἡ ἁγία καὶ οἰκουμενικὴ σύνοδος, ἑτέραν πίστιν μηδενὶ ἐξεῖναι προφέρειν, ἤγουν ουγγράφειν, ἢ συντιθέναι, ἢ φρονεῖν, ἢ διδάσκειν ἑτέρους. τοὺς δὲ τολμῶντας ἢ συντιθέναι πίστιν ἑτέραν, ἤγουν προκομίζειν, ἢ διδάσκειν, ἢ παραδιδόναι ἕτερον σύμβολον τοῖς ἐθέλουσιν ἐπιστρέφειν εἰς ἐπίγνωσιν ἀληθείας ἐξ Ἑλληνισμοῦ, ἢ ἐξ Ἰουδαϊσμοῦ, ἤγουν ἐξ αἱρέσεως οἱασδηποτοῦν, τούτους, εἰ μὲν εἶεν ἐπίσκοποι ἢ κληρικοὶ, ἀλλοτρίους εἶναι τοὺς ἐπισκόπους τῆς ἐπισκοπῆς, καὶ τοὺς κληρικοὺς τοῦ κλήρου· εἰ δὲ μονάζοντες ἢ λαϊκοὶ εἶεν, ἀναθεματίζεσθαι αὐτούς.

[d] Vide Hooker ut supra.

substantial with us according to the Manhood; in all things like unto us without sin; begotten before all ages of the Father according to the Godhead, and in these latter days, for us and for our salvation, born of Mary, the Virgin Mother of God, according to the Manhood; one and the same Christ, Son, Lord, Only-begotten, to be acknowledged in two natures, inconfusedly, unchangeably, indivisibly, inseparably, the distinction of natures being by no means taken away by the union, but rather the property of each nature being preserved, and concurring in one Person and one Subsistence*, not parted or divided into two persons, but one and the same Son, and only-begotten, God the Word, the Lord Jesus Christ, as the Prophets from the beginning have declared concerning Him, and the Lord Jesus Christ Himself has taught us, and the Creed of the holy Fathers has delivered to us.

These things then, being expressed by us with the utmost accuracy and attention, the holy and Œcumenical Synod has decreed that it shall not be lawful for any one to bring forward, or to write, or compose, or devise, or to teach men any other Creed. But those who dare to compose any other Creed, or to bring forward, or teach, or deliver any other Creed to those who are desirous of turning to the acknowledgment of he truth from Heathenism or Judaism, or any heresy whatsoever, if they are Bishops or of the Clergy they shall be deposed, the Bishops from the Episcopate, and the Clergymen from the Clergy; but if they are monks or laymen, they shall be anathematized.

---

* Is here equivalent to *Person*.

ΜΕΤΑ δὲ τὴν ἀνάγνωσιν τοῦ ὅρου πάντες οἱ εὐλαβέστατοι ἐπίσκοποι ἐβόησαν· αὕτη ἡ πίστις τῶν πατέρων. οἱ μητροπολῖται ἄρτι ὑπογράψωσι· παρόντων αὐτῶν ἀρχόντων, ἄρτι ὑπογράψωσι· τὰ καλῶς ὁρισθέντα ὑπέρθεσιν μὴ δέξηται. αὕτη ἡ πίστις τῶν ἀποστίλων· ταύτῃ πάντες στοιχοῦμεν· πάντες οὕτω φρονοῦμεν. οἱ μεγαλοπρεπέστατοι καὶ ἐνδοξότατοι ἄρχοντες εἶπον· τὰ παρὰ τῶν ἁγίων πατέρων τυπωθέντα, καὶ πᾶσιν ἀρέσαντα, δῆλα τῇ θείᾳ γενήσεται κορυφῇ.

ΔΟΞΑ ΕΝ ΥΨΙΣΤΟΙΣ ΘΕΩ ΚΑΙ ΕΠΙ ΓΗΣ
ΕΙΡΗΝΗ.

When the definition of faith had been read, all the most religious Bishops lifted up their voice, and said, "This is the faith of the Fathers. Let the Metropolitans forthwith subscribe it; In the presence of the rulers let them straightway subscribe it. Let not that which hath been rightly defined be delayed. This is the faith of the Apostles; by this rule we all walk: Thus are we all minded." The great men and most illustrious rulers said, "The things that have been defined by the holy Fathers, and have seemed good to all, shall be proclaimed by the appointed supreme power."

"I and my sons and my brethren will walk in the covenant of our fathers. God forbid that we should forsake the law and the ordinances."

INDEX.

ACCUSERS of Bishops and Clergy to be examined, p. 67.
Acolytes, a minor order, 61.
Acts ii. ult., 31.
Alexander of Apamæa, 37; of Hierapolis, 37; Bishop of Alexandria, 5.
Alexandria, jurisdiction of the Bishop, 9.
Anatolius, Archbishop of Constantinople, 75.
Anomæans, 25.
Antioch, John, Bishop of, 37; Church of, reference to its privileges, 27; Canon XX. of the Council referred to, 65; Canon XXIV. of the Council referred to, 67; note on the Synod of, 41.
Apollinarians, 25.
Apostates, discipline to be observed with them, 15.
Apostolic Canon XIV. cited, 53; XL. referred to, 67; XXXVII. referred to, 65.
Apringius of Chalcedon, 37.
Archdeacon, probable origin of the office, 71.
Arians, and Semi-Arians, 25.
Aristeri, the, 31.
Arius, a priest of the Church at Alexandria, 5.
Aurelius of Irenopolis, 39.

Beggars, houses provided for them, 59.
Bingham, Antiquities, xxi. 1, p. 9; iii., xxiii. ii. 1, referred to, 61; vii. 4, referred to, 63.
Bishop, of his jurisdiction over his Clergy, 17.
Bishops not to be degraded to the order of priests, 73; their goods not to be seized, on their decease, by the Clergy, 67; their consecration not to be put off, 69; their jurisdiction to extend to monks, 53; of their appointment, 7; not to excommunicate any rashly, 9; none to be made without consent of the Metropolitan, 9; not to ordain out of their dioceses, 45; concerning their accusers, 29; to keep to their own dioceses, 27; not to be two in one city, 13.
Boniface, priest, at Chalcedon, 75.
Bright, W., reference to his edition of St. Leo's Sermons, &c., 77.

Cælestius, his adherents deposed, 39, 41; a disciple of Pelagius, 41.
Cataphryges, *see* Montanists.
Catechumens, discipline of the lapsed, 17; classes of, *ib.*
Cathari, the, 31.
Catholic faith, the, confirmed by Emperors, 49.
Celestine, of Rome, 83.
Charisius, a priest, 43, 45.
Chorepiscopus, their order and office, 13; distinguished from the Bishop, 49, 50.
Church, unity of the, 9, note.
Churches, their dedication, 55.
Cities, to have every one a bishop, 65.
Clergy, to keep to their own city or parish, 17; regulations respecting ordination and dismissal, 5; their households, 7; not to renounce their calling, 55; to be subject to the Bishop, *ib.*; not to go to law in the

secular courts, 57; to remain in their own place, 53; are not to farm or trade, 51; not to leave their place, 67.
Constantinople, precedence of the Bishop, 27; certain irregularities at, *ib.*; decree of the Council of Chalcedon on the privileges of the See, 71, 73.
1 Corinthians i. 18, p. 31; vi. 1, referred to, 57.
Council of Ephesus, attendance at it enforced, 39.
Councils, imperial influence exercised at, 51; imperial influence in, 73.
Creed, of Constantinople, commonly called Nicene, 35; the Nicene to be exclusively adopted, 43.
Creeds, confirmed at Chalcedon, 79; Nicene, 2, 3; Constantinopolitan, 34, 35.
Cyprus, decree of the Council of Ephesus concerning that province, 45, 47.
Cyril of Alexandria, 83, 87; reference to his Letter against Nestorius, 79.

Damascus, John, Bishop of, 37.
Deaconesses, rules concerning, 63; Paulianist, 21.
Deacons, certain restrictions of their office, 19.
Defensor of the Church, 69.
Diocesan stewards, 71.
Doorkeepers, a minor order, 61.
Dorotheus of Marcianopolis, 37.

Egypt, Case of the Bishops of, 77.
Eliz. I. i. 36, v.
Ephesians ii. 18, p. 31.
Euagrius, Bishop of Soli, 45.
Eucharist, care taken for the worthy celebration of it, 9; not to be administered by deacons, 19.
Eudoxians, 25.

Eunomians, 25.
Eunuchs, 5.
Euphemia, martyr, 55, 81.
Eustathius of Parnassus, 37; Bishop of Berytus, 59, 75; of Antioch, 5.
Euthyrius of Tyana, 37.
Eutyches, a disturber of the Church, 49.
Eutychians, condemned, 85.
Excommunicated, the, are to be subject to discipline, 69.
Excommunicate persons, examination of each case ordered, 7.
Exorcists, a minor order, 61.

Flavian, Archbishop, 87.
Fritilas of Heraclea, 37.

Hebrews v. 10, vii. 1, referred to, 75.
Helladius of Ptolemais, 39; of Tarsus, 37.
Heresies, what so adjudged by law of the Church of England, v.; note on several, 25.
Heretics, definition of the term, 29.; manner of their reconciliation to the Church, 33; of their admission to the Church, 31.
Hesychius of Castabala, 37.
Himerius of Nicomedia, 37.
Homoiousians, 25.
Hooker, R., Eccl. Pol., V. liv. 10, referred to, 85.
Hosius of Corduba, 5.
Hypostasis, the term explained, 89.
Hypostatic union of two natures in the Person of Christ, a consequence of its denial, 41.

S. Irenæus adv. Hær., iii. 8, p. 27.

James of Constantinople, 45.
Jerusalem, precedence of the Bishop, 11.
Johnson, J., "Clergyman's Vade Mecum" referred to, 5.

Jurisdiction, distinct from Orders, 27, note.
Jus, Basilica. I. 1, cited, 49; Corp. Jur. Civ., Nouell. 131. 2, p. 27; Corp. Jur. Civ., Nouell. 123. 32, referred to, 57; Corp. Jur. Civ. Instit. i. 25, Codex V. 62—70, cited, 51; Corp. Jur. Civ., Nouell. 131. 1, cited, 49; Corp. Jur. Civ., Codex IV., xxxii. 26, xxxiii. 2, Digest XXII. ii. 4, p. 19; Corp. Jur. Civ. Instit., ii. 1. 8, cited, 69.
Justinian, Emperor, 49.

Kneeling, forbidden on Sunday and at Pentecost, 21.

Lambeth Conference, 1867, extract from Resolutions, iv.
Laodicæa, Canon ii. of the Council, referred to, 63.
Lapsed, the, not to be ordained, 13; their penance, 13, 15.
Law, Clergy are not to go to law in the secular courts, 57. See *Jus*.
Lent, antiquity of its observance, 9, note.
St. Leo, Archbishop of all the Churches, 79; his influence at the Council of Chalcedon, 73 n., 77; "President of great Rome," 87; reference to "The Tome," 77.
Letters of credence, various sorts of, 59; commendatory, 61.
Lord's Day, prayers to be made standing, 21.
St. Luke i. 8, 9, referred to, 75.

Macarius of Laodicæa, 37.
Macedonius, Bishop of Constantinople, 23, n.
Marcellians, 25.
Marcian, Emperor, 49.
Marcian and Valentinus, the Council of Chalcedon assembled by their ordinance, 81.

Marriages, mixed, of the minor orders forbidden, 61.
Martyries, 55.
St. Mary, the blessed Virgin, the Mother of God, 41, 85; the Virgin Mother of God, 89.
St. Matthew xviii. 8, 9; xix. 12, p. 5.
Maximin of Anazarbus, 37.
Maximus, the Cynic, his acts disallowed, 27.
Meletius, reference to his case, 9; of Neocæsarea, 37.
Metropolitans, their order and jurisdiction, 73; reference to their jurisdiction, 39; to ratify the acts of provincial bishops, 7; antiquity of their authority, 9.
Minor orders, the, 61.
Monasteries, certain rules for their regulation, 53; not to be secularized, 69.
Monks, Canon of Chalcedon concerning them, 53.
Montanists, 31.
"Mother of God," use of the term, 85; note on the term, 41.
Musæus of Aradus, 39.

Nestorians, condemned, 85.
Nestorius, Bishop of Constantinople, 37; his adherents deposed, 39, 41; his acts disallowed, 41.
Nicene decrees ratified, 23, 25, 79.
Novatians, concerning their reconciliation, 11.

Orders, distinct from Jurisdiction, 27, note; not necessarily obliterated by Schism, 11; not to be bought, 49; the minor orders enumerated, 61.
Ordination, none to be ordained without a charge, 55.
Ordination of Clergy, rules to be observed, 5.

INDEX. 95

Parishes, Clergy to keep to their own, 17; Ecclesiastical to follow the civil boundary, 65; rules for country parishes, 63.
Pascasinus, Bishop, legate of Rome, 79.
Patriarch, the rank of, when obtained by the Bishop of Constantinople, 73.
Patripassians, 25.
Paul of Emissa, 37.
Paulianists, discipline to be taken with them on their reconciliation, 21.
Pelagius, 41.
Penance, certain rules of, 13, 15.
Pentecost, prayers to be made standing at, 21.
Philip of Theodosiopolis, 37.
Photinians, 25.
Photius, Bishop of Tyre, 75.
Phryges, see Montanists.
Pluralities, honorary or otherwise, disallowed, 57.
Pneumatomachi, 25.
Polychronius, of Heracleopolis, 37.
Poor-houses, 59.
Prayers, to be made standing at certain days and seasons, 21.
Preferment, not to be bought, 49.
Priests, of those irregularly ordained, 13; their privileges, 19.
Provinces, privileges of certain, 9.
Provincial Synods, to be held twice a-year, 65.

Quarto-decimans, the, 31.

Readers, a minor order, 61.
Reconciliation of heretics, 33.
Rheginus, Bishop of Constantia, 45.
Romans xvi. 1, referred to, 63.
Rome, legates of, at Chalcedon, 49.
Rome, precedence of the Bishop of, 27, 79; primacy of, 73, 79.
Routh, M. J., Opuscula, pp. 470, 1, referred to, 73.
Russian Church, Bishops necessarily monks, 53.

Sabbatius, a heretic, 31.
Sabellians, 25.
Sallustius of Corycus, 37.
Sardica, Canons of Council referred to, 5.
Sardican Decrees, reference to, 29.
Schismatics, regulations as to their reconciliation, 11; definition of the term, 29; to be rebaptized and ordained in certain cases, 21.
Seducers of women and accomplices, their punishment, 71.
Simony, condemned, 49, 51.
Singers, a minor order, 61.
Societies of Clergy against Bishops condemned, 65.
Socrates, Hist. Eccl. ii. 21; Hist. Eccl. ii. 17, referred to, 73.
Sozomen, Hist. Eccl. iii. 10, referred to, 73.
Steward, of the Church, 69, 71.
Subdeacons, a minor order, 61.
Synod, Apostatical, attendance at punished, 39, 41; provincial, consists of Bishops, 63.

Tatian of Augusta, 39.
Tertullian, Q. S. F., de cor. Mil. 3, 4, p. 21; a Montanist, 31.
Tetradites, see Quarto-decimans.
Theodore of Mopsuestia, 43, 45.
Theodoret of Cyrus, 37.
Theodosius, Emperor, letter of the Synod of Constantinople to him, 23.
Theophanes of Philadelphia, 39.
Theotokos, note on the term, 41, 85; see "Mother of God."
1 Tim. v. 17, referred to, 75; vi. 10, referred to, 63.
Title to orders necessary, 55.

Trade, forbidden to the Clergy, 51.
Translations, clerical, rules for those who are translated, 59.

Unions of Clergy against Bishops condemned, 65.
Unity of the Church, 9, note.
Usury, forbidden to the Clergy, 19; legal rate of, *ib.*

Valentinus of Mutoblaca, 37.
Viaticum, the, not to be denied to penitents, 15.
Vincentius, Roman legate, 5.
Virgins, rules concerning them, 63.
Vitus, Roman legate, 5.

Zeno, Bishop of Arium, 45.
Zosys of Esbuns, 37.

www.ingramcontent.com/pod-product-compliance
Lightning Source LLC
Chambersburg PA
CBHW030436190426
43202CB00036B/1568